MICHAEL CAINE

'YOU'RE A BIG MAN...'

For Philippa, thank you for your patience, love, and encouragement.

MICHAEL CAINE

'YOU'RE A BIG MAN...'

THE PERFORMANCES THAT MADE THE ICON

MATTHEW FIELD

BT BATSFORD

First Published 2003

Text © Livonia Productions Ltd 2003

The right of Matthew Field to be identified as Author of this work has been
asserted by him in accordance with the Copyright, Designs and Patents Act 1988.

Design by Neil Stevens

Picture research by Zoe Holtermann

Volume © B T Batsford

ISBN 07134 8876 X

A CIP catalogue record for this book is available from the British Library.

Printed in Spain
for the publishers
B T Batsford
Chrysalis Books Group
The Chrysalis Building
Bramley Road
London W10 6SP
www.batsford.com

Distributed in the United States and Canada by Sterling Publishing
Co., 387 Park Avenue South, New York, NY 10016, USA

An imprint of Chrysalis Books Group plc

Contents

Foreword by Michael Caine

'So this is what I've been doing for the last forty-five years.'

It's a surprise and a delight for me to have this book because it is a chronicle of what I've been doing rather than a biography, which, after all, is only the opinion and view of a single man. But this book lets you, the reader, make up your mind about what I am and what the hell I've been up to all this time.

Although I have photos of myself at 6 months, 6 years, 11 years and 18 years, it's not a great photographic chronicle of my early life. This book, with its excellent choice of photos, shows that I've more than made up for that shortfall.

Matthew's research is excellent and if you're at all interested in me or my career, then I recommend this book wholeheartedly. It's fair comment, which is unusual in my professional life.

Michael Caine

25th August 2003

Introduction
Citizen Caine

From Palmer to Powers, from Italy to Newcastle, the former Maurice Micklewhite has become the London lad done good. As Barry Norman once suggested: if you add it up, maybe only one in seven of Michael Caine's hundred-odd films is actually worth seeing, yet he has become one of the world's best-loved movie stars. Productivity rather than quality is Caine's motto it would seem, when it comes to his career. He once said, 'First of all I choose the great roles, and if none of those come, I choose the mediocre ones, and if none of those come, I choose the ones that pay the rent.'

Born Maurice Joseph Micklewhite in March 1933 in South London, it was after undergoing his National Service in Korea in 1952 that he decided he wanted to pursue a career in acting. Changing his name to Michael Scott, he was told by his agent that Equity already had an actor by that name on their books, and was forced to change it for a second time. Gazing up at the billboard in London's Leicester Square for the film *The Caine Mutiny* his mind was made up: Michael Caine.

> **First of all I choose the great roles, and if none of those come, I choose the mediocre ones, and if none of those come, I choose the ones that pay the rent**

Caine is perhaps the best-loved and most popular British actor in the world, becoming one of Britain's few memorable international movie stars. Many told him he could never be an actor because he didn't talk posh. His reaction was: 'I'll show them how to be an actor without talking posh ... and I did!' But it wasn't until the age of 30, and after spending years as a struggling actor, that Caine hit the big time.

Zulu transformed Caine into a movie star. It was a film packed with spectacle: stunning photography, brilliant editing and a spine-tingling soundtrack. It embraced the kind of heroism that would stir the blood of generations after it.

With the mighty success of *Zulu* behind him, James Bond producer Harry Saltzman gave Caine the lead in *The Ipcress File*: secret agent Harry Palmer, a character who was the complete antithesis of 007. Caine even insisted on wearing his black horn-rimmed glasses for the part, claiming '... no leading man had worn glasses in a film since Harold Lloyd!'

Alfie is one of the most talked about films of the 1960s. The frank discussion of pre-marital sex and adultery combined with the chirpy cockney banter may seem a little dated now, but Caine as the womanizing lothario must rank as one of his strongest performances of all. Caine was nominated for his first Academy Award for the movie, but lost out to Paul Scofield in *A Man For All Seasons*. *Alfie* was the swinging Sixties on film, and Caine's cockney accent is showcased with no apologies, something he is proud about, although he feels he has been patronized by the British press. He said 'I'm every bourgeois nightmare: a cockney with intelligence and a million dollars.'

After a spate of forgettable movies Caine left the Sixties in style as Charlie Croker in Peter Collinson's *The Italian Job*. This piece of patriotic cinema, told in a typically Sixties jingoistic fashion, benefited from a fantastic array of cameo performers from such comedians as Benny Hill and Fred Emney. But it was the appearance of three Mini Coopers in a fender-bending car chase through the streets and arcades of Turin that stole the show from Caine. 'It was the greatest advert for the Mini the world has ever seen,' he comments. The fact that Hollywood has recently remade *The Italian Job* does nothing but beg the question 'Why?'

Michael Caine was a British icon by the Seventies. After appearing in the all-star cast of *The Battle of Britain*, Caine portrayed Jack Carter in the Mike Hodges' film *Get Carter*, a film that sealed his reputation as the number one gangster in British cinema. It was this movie that became the genesis of the gangster genre, the film that spawned *Lock Stock* and *Snatch* et al.

Throughout the Sixties Caine lived the life of a playboy. He shared a flat with Terence Stamp, and they indulged themselves in a world of fast cars, fashion and girls. But in 1972 he spotted the love of his life in a television commercial for Maxwell House coffee. Shakira Baksh became Mrs Caine in Las Vegas: 'It was like one of those weddings you see in a corny movie. My agent gave the bride away and paid for the wedding. It was only $174.'

Not long after finishing *Get Carter*, Caine was faced with what is arguably his most challenging role to date – *Sleuth*, in which he appeared opposite Laurence Olivier. 'I realise I have a partner,' commented a shrewd Olivier just weeks into filming. Both actors were nominated for an Oscar for best actor, but neither walked away with the coveted award, which instead went to Marlon Brando for *The Godfather*.

In 1975 Caine made his favourite movie of all time *The Man Who Would Be King*, in which he starred opposite his old chum Sean Connery. For both actors, making the film was one of their most enjoyable experiences of all time. *The Man Who Would Be King*, directed by John Huston, even found room for a cameo performance for Caine's wife Shakira.

In the mid-Seventies Caine decided it was time to quit England. Fed up with the amount he was paying in taxes he became a tax exile in California. He was vocal in his irritation, claiming he was being penalized for his own success. He later said that his talent was appreciated more in the States: 'In America I'm treated as a skilled movie actor. Here I'm a cockney yobbo who was in the right place at the right time.'

Upon his arrival across the Atlantic, he indulged in a string of big-budget disaster movies. *The Swarm*, *Beyond The Poseidon Adventure* and *Ashanti* were disasters in every sense of the word.

After this period of poor-quality films, *Educating Rita* was firm evidence of Caine's acting ability. It was just so completely different from anything he had ever done before. Putting on two stone in weight and growing a face full of hair, Caine hobbled around the streets of Dublin as a drunk university professor of English Literature, as he reluctantly taught Julie Walters the finer points of poetry and Shakespeare. Caine's performance earned him yet another Oscar nomination, but once again the gold-plated statue eluded him.

After *Educating Rita* the gems seemed to dry up, although one small movie entitled *Deathtrap*, in which Caine co-starred with Christopher Reeve, did test his limits as an actor. A series of disasters ensued: *Blame It On Rio*, *The Honorary Consul* and *Water*. Some suggested that his time was up. One British columnist commented that he was corny and clichéd and had '…been coasting along on a very small talent for a very long time'. But he was still commanding big money, and was one of only a handful of Brits who had the respect of the major Hollywood studios, and his first Oscar was just around the corner.

By the mid-Eighties the razzmatazz of Hollywood had lost its savour for Caine and he returned to England with his family.

Hannah And Her Sisters was by no means as good a role as *Educating Rita*, but it did give him the opportunity to work with the great Woody Allen. This collaboration brought that most coveted prize: an Oscar (for Best Supporting Actor). With the Oscar firmly in his hands he said, 'This little fellow is the big one. It's another dream come true.' But every silver lining has a cloud, and Caine confessed that he was a little disappointed, 'I'd rather have won it for *Educating Rita* – I really thought I was going to win that one.'

After he had finally won the Oscar he made another run of nonsense: *Without A Clue*, *The Fourth Protocol* and one of his most famous stinkers of all time, *Jaws: The Revenge*. He was offered a tremendous fee and he took the job. One film that stood out among the dross was *Mona Lisa*, which required Caine to slip on his gangster shoes once more as he performed a cameo role as a hard-nut killer opposite Bob Hoskins. Caine claims he had never been so sure about a part before or since.

Caine had always had a hankering to direct but in 1988 admitted that maybe that fad had passed: 'I have reached that stage that if I have any spare time I like to fill it at the Hotel du Cap in the south of France or somewhere. So the thought of getting up at 6 in the morning to direct a load of buggers like me is not as attractive as it was.'

In 1988 the wonderful *Dirty Rotten Scoundrels* appeared. He starred opposite Steve Martin, with the duo playing a couple of crooks working on the French Riviera. However, this was again followed by a string of disasters, including

Michael Winner's *Bullseye!* with Roger Moore. Yet at Christmas 1992 Caine reappeared in a role that was both a surprise and a treat. Playing Ebenezer Scrooge opposite Miss Piggy in *The Muppet Christmas Carol*, Caine gave his best performance for years and visibly enjoyed the whole filmmaking process.

For a while, during the early Nineties, Caine took a break from the game. His dissatisfaction with making movies left him time to write his autobiography. He also used the hiatus to open a string of restaurants. He had for some time had a share in the famous Langans, the 'in' place in London's Mayfair, and knew his wines as well as he knew his scripts.

'I've made a lot of crap and a lot of money, which means I can afford to be artistic now,' he said after completing a small picture entitled *Little Voice* in 1998. After several years out of the game Michael Caine came back with a bang. *Little Voice* was blessed with the wonderful British cast of Ewan MacGregor, Jane Horrocks, Brenda Blethyn and Jim Broadbent, and was the first of a string of good movies and great roles for Caine. He was on a roll.

With the lad-magazine boom of the Nineties, Caine's iconic status was reborn. He was increasingly popular with the new generation of young British men, who found much to admire in the lothario Alfie, the crime mastermind in *The Italian Job* and the gangster of *Get Carter*. As *Get Carter* inspired a new wave of popular, successful Brit-flick gangster movies, a fresh generation of British youth discovered a young Michael Caine.

The good roles kept coming and his next choice was to be one of his best yet: Dr Larch in *The Cider House Rules* (1999). 'He is probably the nicest and gentlest person I have ever played,' said Caine shortly after the film was released. Set in the Thirties, *The Cider House Rules* was the passionate story of a doctor's work at an orphanage in New England. It was the movie that earned him his second Oscar.

With the acceptance of his second Academy Award Caine was more in vogue than ever. 'This last Oscar was much more important than the first, because I'd been away. And neither of them were for playing cockneys', he said. But it would turn out to be a double whammy, as on his return to the UK just weeks later, he was presented with Britain's highest accolade, the BAFTA Fellowship award. But nobody was prepared for the ear-bashing rant that was to follow, as he stood on stage in the confines of the Odeon Leicester Square. He told a shocked audience, 'I never felt I belonged in my own country, in my profession, I think of myself as a loner. All the way through I have felt on the outside as though I was trying to make something for myself with very little help.' Some critics didn't care for Caine's tirade, one even stating, 'Poor old Michael Caine, multi-millionaire, Oscar winner, businessman, country estate in Britain, married to one of the world's most beautiful women, and still he's bitter.'

But maybe just someone was listening. In November 2000 he went into Buckingham Palace and emerged as Sir Michael Caine.

Caine burst into the 21st century with an array of splendid roles ranging across the genres: from gangster pictures like *Shiner* to Hollywood comedy *Miss Congeniality* and a retro role in *Austin Powers in Goldmember*. Michael Caine was back.

Caine sums up his career spanning a huge 50 years in one simple statement: 'Usually you have to die to become an icon. I just got there early.'

Matthew Field
April 2003

Early Days

Maurice Micklewhite dreamed of being in the movies while growing up on the poor streets of the Elephant and Castle in London. Leaving school at the age of 15, he found work as a messenger boy on Wardour Street, working for the J Arthur Rank Organisation. But this early flirtation with the movie world was short-lived when he was sacked for smoking in the toilets.

Called up for military service in Korea at the age of 18, he returned home two years later hoping to begin a career in acting, unwilling to follow in his father's footsteps slumming it as a porter in the Billingsgate fish market. 'It was in Korea that I noticed heroes weren't always six feet three with perfectly capped teeth, but ordinary guys,' he said.

Called a sissy and a 'nancy' by those back in the Elephant, he roamed around London's West End with a copy of *The Stage* wedged under his arm in the hope that somebody would notice him. Changing his name to Michael Scott, he fought for work as a TV extra, before going into repertory where he appeared in over 80 plays.

In 1956 he landed his first role in a feature film. *A Hill In Korea* starred Stanley Baker. It was a minor role; in fact it was so minor he didn't even receive a credit. The director, Julian Amyes, gave the young hopeful the part of a soldier with four lines. 'I regarded Michael as a very competent young actor,' he recalls. Others disagreed. On seeing the movie his agent, Jimmy Fraser, dropped him from his books. The reason? He didn't like his blonde eyelashes.

Having been told by Equity that there was already an actor called Michael Scott he needed to find a new professional name. After being inspired by the poster for a new movie of the time, *The Caine Mutiny*, he chose the name that would become famous. After continuing to take small 'blink-and-you-miss-him' parts, he finally received his first screen credit in Nigel Patrick's *How To Marry A Rich Uncle* in 1957.

Zulu was still a long way off. He struggled his way through the late Fifties taking brief roles whenever and wherever he could get them. He continued to make fleeting appearances in such movies as *Danger*

Within, The Key, Passport To Shame and _Foxhole In Cairo_. In _Solo For Sparrow_ he played an Irish gangster, but on the first day the producer heard Caine's attempt at an Irish accent and wouldn't let him say another line in the film.

The television play _The Compartment_ (1963) was unwittingly tailor-made for Caine: the story of two men in a railway carriage, one a middle-class snob, the other, as Caine puts it, 'a vulgar cockney'. In fact, agent Dennis Selinger placed Caine on his books simply on the strength of this one performance. Shortly after the screening of the play, Caine was stopped by Roger Moore as he walked down Piccadilly. Moore, who by 1962 had become famous as The Saint, stopped Caine to shake his hand and congratulate him on his performance.

Then there was _Zulu_. The rest, as they say, is history. He had certainly deserved the break, after more than 150 television plays and over 10 years as a penniless struggling actor. During those early difficult days, Michael had said to himself, 'Michael, you're never going to become a star. You've not got much personality. So what you've got to do is learn how to act.' He did become a star, with a strong personality, and demonstrated repeatedly the quality of his talent.

Early Filmography

Sailor Beware	1956
A Hill In Korea	1956
How To Murder A Rich Uncle	1957
The Steel Bayonet	1957
Carve Her Name With Pride	1958
The Key	1958
The Two-Headed Spy	1958
Passport To Shame	1958
Danger Within	1958
The Bulldog Breed	1960
Foxhole In Cairo	1960
The Day The Earth Caught Fire	1961
The Wrong Arm Of The Law	1962
Solo For Sparrow	1962

Note that all the films in this book are ordered by the year of their release and NOT by the year of production.

Zulu

(1964)

War drama UK Colour 138 mins

Stanley Baker, Michael Caine,
Jack Hawkins, Ulla Jacobsson
James Booth

Director: Cy Endfield
Producers: Stanley Baker/Cy Endfield
Screenplay: John Prebble and
Cy Endfield

For Michael Caine, *Zulu* was a long time coming, but when it did, his career and life hit the fast lane.

Cy Endfield's superb re-creation of the 1879 battle at Rorke's Drift provided a stunning star-making performance for Caine. But it was only by chance that the then 'jobbing' actor landed the role of Gonville Bromhead opposite the legendary Stanley Baker, who also acted as the film's producer. 'You don't look like a cockney to me. You look more like an officer. Can you do an officer's accent?' asked Cy. Caine could do anything, and immediately screen-tested for the role of the foppish lieutenant. He landed the part on the eve of his 30th birthday, the date Caine vowed he would give up acting unless he found a break. Bumping into the actor at a party, Endfield told Caine, 'It was the worst screen test I've ever seen, but you got the part … don't ask me why.' Caine later found out that there was no time to find anyone else, and within days

an entire production unit flew out to South Africa to begin work on one of Michael Caine's most famous performances of all time.

Once Caine had been offered the part of the lieutenant, he painstakingly researched the life of the real Bromhead, who had

> **He painstakingly researched the life of the real Bromhead, who had been short, dark and partially deaf**

been short, dark and partially deaf. Michael persuaded both Baker and Endfield to allow him to show hidden strength in the

character, who, in the script, appeared merely as an ineffectual Victorian officer. He suggested that if the character were to be more complex it would reflect better on Baker's character John Chard.

Much of the film's joy comes from the stunning photography of the battle scenes and the Zulus en masse. The sequences of the Zulus thundering over the mountain are truly spectacular. Add to that the bright red tunics and white helmets of the Royal Engineers against a backdrop of blue skies and the scenery of Rorke's Drift and you can see why the film still thrills to this day. John Barry's haunting soundtrack and Richard Burton's narration were the icing on the cake. But filmmaking was a new experience for the Zulus: the African extras had never seen a film before, let alone acted in one. The real Zulu leader Chief Buthelesi was even playing Chief Cetewayo in the film. To give the Zulus a taste of Hollywood, Baker's crew painted a

gigantic rock white, which became the screen for nightly projected performances of Buster Keaton and Laurel and Hardy, shown to a bemused 4,000-strong crowd.

Caine remembers the early days of filming with some unease: 'I was so nervous on those first few takes, it still makes me shudder.' As he recalls: 'It was a boiling hot day. I was speaking in an accent which, to say the least, was absolutely unnatural, very upper crust and

old school. And I was on a horse that didn't like me.' Caine is famous for not viewing his rushes, but made an exception at this early stage in *Zulu*: 'I was sick on the floor. Someone from Paramount had already sent a telegram from London suggesting I should be replaced'. Producer Joseph E Levine had his

own thoughts on Caine's performance. Calling the actor into his office, he said, 'I've seen the picture. You look gay, you look like a homosexual ... You'll never be a star, you're butch but you look like a fag.' How wrong can a man be? But co-star Jack Hawkins saw the writing on the wall: 'There is a new young actor in it called Michael Caine. Look out for him because he's going to become a star.'

"You'll never be a star, you're butch but you look like a fag "

The Ipcress File

(1965)

Spy thriller UK Colour 102 mins

Michael Caine, Nigel Green,
Guy Doleman, Sue Lloyd,
Gordon Jackson, Aubrey Richards,
Frank Gatliff, Thomas Baptiste,
Oliver MacGreevy, Freda Bamford

Director: Sidney J Furie

Producer: Harry Saltzman

Screenplay: Bill Canaway, from
the novel by Len Deighton

The Ipcress File was the first of three films in which Caine portrayed the secret agent Harry Palmer, a character created by novelist Len Deighton.

With the success of *Zulu*, Caine was inundated with offers. The most serious of these was from Harry Saltzman, the co-producer of the James Bond films. 'I thought I was going to replace Sean,' jokes Caine. Saltzman was looking to create a character that was the complete antithesis of 007, an agent who wore horn-rimmed glasses and cooked his own food, something the cool Connery would never be seen doing. Palmer was a glamourized version of the real secret agent. 'We decided to have Harry Palmer in a supermarket pushing his own trolley. Here was territory that Bond, brave though he was, had never trodden.' The decision for the character to wear glasses in the film was an important and hard decision. As Caine recalls: 'No leading man had worn glasses in a film. People said he can't cook they'll think he's gay, he can't wear glasses they'll think he's a sissy.' It was during a meal at the famous Sixties Pickwick Club that Caine signed for the role. Saltzman asked Michael if he was aware of a spy novel entitled *The Ipcress File*. By sheer coincidence Caine was reading the book at the time. The Canadian movie mogul

"AN ADMIRABLE THRILLER IN EVERY RESPECT!"

"A THINKING MAN'S 'GOLDFINGER', FUNNIER BY FAR THAN ANY OF THE BOND FILMS AND MORE REWARDING, TOO!"

HARRY SALTZMAN presents

THE IPCRESS FILE

From the teachers best seller by LEN DEIGHTON

starring

MICHAEL CAINE

with starring NIGEL GREEN · GUY DOLEMAN · SUE LLOYD

Produced by HARRY SALTZMAN · Directed by SIDNEY J. FURIE · CHARLES KASHER

Screenplay by BILL CANAWAY & JAMES DORAN · Music composed and conducted by JOHN BARRY

TECHNICOLOR® TECHNISCOPE® A UNIVERSAL RELEASE

Sidney J Furie, who adopted a style of filmmaking that proved hugely influential, shooting fight sequences through telephone boxes or car windows, and using a host of other obscure and gimmicky camera angles. But Furie was apparently not happy with the original screenplay, and on the first day of shooting is reported to have set fire to the script, throwing it to the floor in front of Caine and asking what he should do. But the young director elicited sterling performances not only from Michael Caine but also his co-stars Nigel Green and Guy Doleman.

The Ipcress File was a new kind of spy movie. The plot was complex and confusing in places, and Furie's work has a particular mood, especially once mixed with Peter Hunt's fast-paced editing and John Barry's intriguing score. In Caine's words the film had a certain 'ambience' about it. The use of London locations, including the Albert Hall, enhanced the

public image of Caine as a Londoner, very much a part of the Sixties London scene. The critics adored Caine's performance. With his first leading role behind him, Michael Caine had become a movie star.

> "**...for the first time I heard the phrase 'hundred thousand pounds,'...thinking what a wonderful language English really was**"

offered him a seven-year contract on the spot. 'He talked about my seven-year contract in numbers that I could not comprehend. All I can remember was that they were longer than telephone numbers, and for the first time I heard the phrase 'hundred thousand pounds,' and sat there bewildered and thinking what a wonderful language English really was.'

Shot at Pinewood Studios, the film was directed by Canadian

Alfie

(1966)

Comedy drama UK Colour 109 mins

Michael Caine, Shelly Winters,
Millicent Martin, Julia Foster,
Jane Asher, Shirley Anne Field,
Vivien Merchant, Eleanor Bron,
Denholm Elliott, Alfie Bass
Director/Producer: Lewis Gilbert
Screenplay: Bill Naughton from
his play

Based on the radio play by Bill Naughton, *Alfie* became one of the most talked about movies of the Sixties. Its frank discussion of pre-marital sex and adultery were a revelation to the audience. Although superficially the movie seemed nothing more than a London lothario tearing around London with a flock of girls, the film has dark undertones: the harrowing, unsympathetic abortion scene gave the film great depth and gave Caine a challenge.

Directed by Lewis Gilbert, the black comedy featured a host of dolly birds, including Jane Asher, Shirley Ann Field, Julia Foster and Shelly Winters. In the opening sequence, Caine confidently leaps from a steamed-up parked car, turns to the camera and says, 'My name is Alfie. I suppose you think you're gonna see the bleedin' titles now, well, you're not so you can all relax.' Caine, with his gift of the gab and cockney banter, delivered one of his most popular performances, in particular his

face-to-camera monologues that displayed both charm and naivety. Alfie was someone that audiences should have hated, but Caine played the part with enough depth that the audience took the trouble to try to understand the dynamics of the character. Almost a victim of his own success, Caine created a caricature that was to haunt him for the rest of his career. No matter how far he stretched his acting ability, Alfie and his one-liners would always be lurking in the shadows.

Michael Caine was careful not to become associated too closely with his on-screen character. He said during the film's publicity campaign: 'Most people will associate Alfie with Caine. But I'm not Alfie. He's a disgusting character, criminal in the way he behaves and treats people. I don't deny it too much, because I know he's some sort of confessional for lots of fellows. I knew him, I played him. I'm part of him, but I'm not Alfie,' he stressed.

'The role was turned down by every actor in England,' recalls Caine. Before he accepted Lewis Gilbert's offer he reportedly spent 45 minutes on the phone trying to persuade his flat-mate Terence Stamp to take the part. When Caine did decide to take the part he was astonished at the fee he was offered: 'Lewis Gilbert asked me "Do you want a percentage or a lot of money?" I said, "I want a lot of money." He offered me a sum I never dreamed of, actually 75 thousand dollars, and that cost me about three million dollars'.

Paramount were very anxious about the film before release, their biggest anxiety being Michael's accent, fearing the American audience would not understand what he was saying. One studio executive even suggested that they dub him. But *Alfie* proved an instant hit in America. Costing only £350,000 to make, the film took £10 million at the US box office alone. In fact the Americans loved the film so much that Caine was nominated for an Oscar in the category of best actor.

> **I knew him, I played him. I'm part of him, but I'm not Alfie**

Gambit

(1966)

Crime comedy US Colour 108 mins

Shirley MacLaine, Michael Caine,
Herbert Lom, Roger C Carmel,
Arnold Moss

Director: Ronald Neame

Producer: Leo L Fuchs

Screenplay: Alvin Sargent and Jack
Davies, from the novel by Sidney Carroll

This glossy, cosmopolitan heist movie is often overlooked, buried among the early cult films (and the later stinkers) of Caine's career.

American actress Shirley MacLaine had already signed to star in *Gambit* and apparently had enough clout to choose both her director and leading man. 'She saw *The Ipcress File* and chose me,' says Caine. *Gambit* was written for Cary Grant, but the actor had long since retired and Caine enjoyed being chosen for a part intended for a Hollywood legend.

Directed by Englishman Ronald Neame, *Gambit* sees Caine as Harry Deane, a cockney con man who teams up with MacLaine's character to steal a priceless Egyptian statuette from the penthouse of millionaire Shahbandar (Herbert Lom). The film shows us the story twice: first the 'ideal' version as conceived in Caine's mind, with MacLaine as a silent follower and Lom as closet recluse, and second the reality as the heist unfolds.

Gambit was the first film Michael Caine made in America: 'Hollywood was better than I had ever dreamed it would be. I was a massive film fan and I was introduced to everyone in Hollywood.' Caine's arrival in the US was greeted enthusiastically, with one critic commenting: 'Well girls, first we had the Beatles and then it was miniskirts, and now see what the British have sent us in the way of flicks – a cockney lad who's sure to be our cup of tea.'

His co-star Shirley MacLaine remembers his arrival: 'He tickled me with his dry, sardonic wit … He cut a swathe through the single girls in Hollywood like a rocket with no resistance. He'd report for work after a hard night's play, stagger into his trailer, blast his Beatles records up to hyperspace, and try to get some sleep.'

Both impressed and dazzled by tinsel town, Caine recalls the difficulties the location caused: 'The movie was being short in the [Los Angeles] valley, which was notorious for its smog. Sometimes it was so thick you couldn't see a hundred yards in front of you, and it stung the eyes.' Although LA was the main location, some of the movie was shot in exotic Hong Kong, the setting for the first half of the story.

Gambit was a fun experience for all involved, as Caine recalls in his memoirs: '*Gambit* was proceeding so smoothly that it became secondary to the incredible social life I was leading. Ronald Neame, the director, was an expert at this light, frothy comedy, Shirley and I worked harmoniously together and Herbert Lom, who was the other star of the movie, was an expert and a sweetheart.'

> He cut a swathe
> through the single
> girls in Hollywood

Funeral In Berlin

(1966)

Spy drama UK Colour 97 mins

Michael Caine, Eva Renzi,
Paul Hubschmid, Oscar Homolka,
Guy Doleman, Rachel Gurney,
Hugh Burden
Director: Guy Hamilton
Producer: Harry Saltzman
Screenplay: Evan Jones, from
the novel by Len Deighton

Now under contract with Harry Saltzman, Michael Caine followed up his successful performance as Harry Palmer in *The Ipcress File* with *Funeral In Berlin*. *Goldfinger* director Guy Hamilton came fresh from the Bond set to tackle Len Deighton's second Palmer novel. Harry goes behind the Iron Curtain to persuade Communist spy boss Oscar Homolka to defect, only to run into Israeli agent Eva Renzi, who is busy tracking down Nazi criminals.

The plot and storyline have often been described as foggy and more than a little unclear, but Caine had grown more than confident in the role and had a strong on-screen presence, even when the rest of the movie failed to deliver. 'I love the character', said Caine during filming. 'And no matter how many times I play Harry Palmer he is my safety valve. He's the chap who keeps me from being typecast.' But times change. Caine signed a contract with Saltzman for seven

Harry Palmer films, and after only three was begging to be released.

Caine compared his secret agent to that of Sean Connery's Bond: 'He played James Bond in his regular style, without any special make-up or costume and that's who he is off screen too. He had to grow a Clark Gable moustache and do a picture like *The Hill* to get away from the Bond image. I put on eye-glasses and a rumpled suit and I'm Harry

Palmer. However, unless I put on those glasses and that suit I'm Michael Caine.'

The film was shot in West Berlin when the city was still divided by the Cold War, and the location is clearly remembered by Caine: 'Every time we tried to film near the wall the Russians used to bring lights and mirrors out and shine them straight into the [camera] lense.' Caine loved the mystery of the city, but felt that the movie didn't quite capture the atmosphere as well as it should.

Although Caine was pleased with the finished picture the critics disagreed. Gone were the plaudits received for *The Ipcress File*, and in their place complaints that the film lacked the pace and style created by its predecessor. Hamilton's interpretation of a Harry Palmer mission did not include the crazy camera angles that Sidney J Furie had adopted with the original.

" I put on eye-glasses and a rumpled suit and I'm Harry Palmer "

Hurry Sundown

(1967)

Drama Colour 145 mins

Michael Caine, Jane Fonda,
John Philip Law, Faye Dunaway,
Robert Hooks, Beah Richards,
George Kennedy,
Burgess Meredith, Diahann Carroll,
Rex Ingram, Peter Goff,
Loring Smith, Luke Askew,
Madeline Sherwood

Director/Producer: Otto Preminger

Screenplay: Thomas C Ryan and
Horton Foote, from the novel by KB
Gilden

"Some critics said I was miscast"

Some critics felt that Caine was totally miscast as a ruthless southerner in this post-World War II melodrama set in Georgia. In *Hurry Sundown* heartless Henry Warren (Caine) tries to buy up the tracts of land that border his property, part of the land being owned by his cousin and part by a black man. The struggle for the land triggers a chain of events that end in tragedy.

The movie was in fact filmed in Louisiana, and racism and segregation became a problem during the course of the shoot. The producers had to obtain special permission to allow the black and white cast members to stay in the same hotel. It was reported that at one stage the Klu Klux Klan fired a gun at director Otto Preminger's trailer while on location.

The Austrian-born director had a reputation for shouting at his actors, although he says this never occurred with Caine: 'I only shout at bad actors … I would never shout at Alfie'. However, Caine emerged from the *Hurry Sundown* experience declaring: 'Otto goes stark raving mad. Rather than sacrificing the actors, he tries to prove he is one'. Time has not mellowed Caine's feelings about the director. In 1992 Caine told *Time Out* magazine, 'He was nice to me but I didn't know how nasty he was to everyone else. He was particularly nasty to Faye Dunaway and I pulled him on that. My attitude was if he says anything to me I'll fucking deck him.'

Even without a volatile director, the role of Henry Warren presented Caine with two challenges: firstly he had to learn how to play the saxophone convincingly and secondly he was required, for the first time ever, to use an American accent. Vivien Leigh reportedly spent several weeks teaching him how to say 'four-door Ford'. *Hurry Sundown* also provided Caine with the opportunity to bed Jane Fonda, at least on screen, with a scene in which he rips off her clothes, down to her bra and knickers, and forces himself on her. Preminger gave Caine one instruction on set: come in the door, go to the bed and rape her.

Caine had his own thoughts on the movie's failure. As he told journalist William Hall in *Arise Sir Michael Caine*, 'Some critics said I was miscast. Personally, I think I took on more than I could chew. I'll tell you why: I was very tired. I had finished filming *Funeral In Berlin*, and now I was in Louisiana, filming in a different accent, and I just pushed myself too far.' Caine also felt he was having difficulty shaking off the ghost of Alfie, fearing he was slowly becoming typecast as the London lothario. 'I never lived that character down until *Sleuth*,' was Caine's view.

Hurry Sundown was quickly buried, with many critics hailing it as a total waste of a staggering talent – maybe they were right.

Billion Dollar Brain

(1967)

Spy thriller UK Colour 104 mins

Michael Caine, Karl Malden,
Francoise Dorleac, Oscar Homolka,
Ed Begley

Director: Ken Russell

Producer: Harry Saltzman

Screenplay: John McGrath, from
the novel by Len Deighton

Billion Dollar Brain saw the conclusion of the Harry Palmer series, for the time being anyway. It was certainly the most 'off-the-wall' of the Palmer films and closer to the James Bond movies with its dynamic sets and futuristic plot. This time the spy travels to Finland to infiltrate Ed Begley's power-crazed organization and – originally – prevent him from taking over the world.

Sitting in the director's chair was Ken Russell, who landed the job on Michael's recommendation: '*Billion Dollar Brain* is a highly complicated thriller, which needs a draftsman,' said Caine during production. Russell made Caine do as much of his own stunt work as possible, including jumping onto ice floes out in the Baltic Sea. 'He was very brave … I wouldn't have done it,' reflects the director. The situation was dangerous: Michael hadn't been supplied with any equipment in case he slipped and fell off the ice floe into the freezing waters. He wouldn't have been able to get out. 'I was just listening to him, because he's fucking crazy and doesn't care about anybody,' joked Caine about his persuasive director. In another close encounter Caine was about to leap onto the running board of a moving train when he noticed the ice hadn't been cleared away from the board. 'I screamed at him [the technician] for about an hour. I didn't do the scene at all. I wouldn't jump it. It was a sheet of solid ice.'

Starring opposite Caine was French actress Françoise Dorleac, the sister of Catherine Deneuve. It was her last film performance, as shortly before filming wrapped she was killed in a car accident on the outskirts of Nice. Caine's own brother Stanley also featured in the film in a cameo performance as a postman. He later went on to play one of Charlie Croker's crooks in *The Italian Job* but acting was never Stanley's destiny and his celluloid career ended with *The Italian Job*.

Billion Dollar Brain looked stylish and lavish, even down to the titles. Saltzman drafted in graphic designer Maurice Binder, who had been responsible for many of the James Bond title sequences, to create similar magic with Palmer. The result was a sequence packed with computer keyboards and

" **Russell made Caine do as much of his own stunt work as possible, including jumping onto ice floes out in the Baltic Sea** "

recurring images of Michael Caine. Combined with Richard Rodney Bennett's score it produced a sense of intrigue.

However, the critics announced they'd had enough of Deighton's hero, showering *Billion Dollar Brain* with disappointing reviews. Although Caine stood up for the picture, saying 'A lot of it was very beautifully directed', which it was, it failed to live up to Sidney Furie's original.

The Italian Job

(1969)

Crime comedy thriller UK

Colour 95 mins

Michael Caine, Noel Coward,

Benny Hill, Raf Vallone,

Tony Beckley

Director: Peter Collinson

Producer: Michael Deeley

Screenplay: Troy Kennedy Martin

> **Paramount...wanted an American lead, suggesting Robert Redford for the part...**

Mix together a band of lovable crooks, three Mini Coopers, a chase through a Turin traffic jam, a busload of gold bullion with Michael Caine, and you have the comedy caper of all time. *The Italian Job*, which is known to millions mainly on the back of multiple bleary-eyed, Boxing Day-screenings, has become a cherished part of British popular culture, embedding itself quite firmly in the nation's psyche.

Directed by Peter Collinson, the film boasts an impressive cast: Michael Caine as Charlie Croker, the perfect embodiment of cool Britannia; Noel Coward as the aristocratic crime lord Mr Bridger; and Benny Hill, with a delicious penchant for extra large ladies. But it was the Mini Cooper that became the star of the show. Sporting the livery of the Union Jack, the three Minis feature in the famous car chase over and under the streets, rooftops and sewers of Turin, which alone has secured the film's place in cinematic history. Producer Michael Deeley realized that the spectacular car chase was going to require the talent of a very skilful stunt team. It's ironic to note that considering how unashamedly patriotic *The Italian Job* is, the vehicle action was actually handled by L'Equipe Remy Julienne, a French team who could barely utter a word of English. 'We knew once we saw Remy doing his stuff, that we had something that maybe people hadn't seen before,' says Caine.

Screenwriter Troy Kennedy Martin of *Z-Cars* fame envisaged nobody except Michael Caine for the lead role, constructing the script around him before he had even signed. Paramount had other ideas: they wanted an American lead, suggesting Robert Redford for the part, but Troy insisted on Caine. The Mr Bridger role was immediately offered to Noel Coward. Working with Coward is probably Caine's fondest memory of the picture: 'We became very

good friends; we used to have dinner at the Savoy every Wednesday, it was probably the most English thing I ever did.'

The production company presumed that BMC, the makers of the Mini, would be thrilled about the Paramount movie, which, shown right across the world, made heroes out of three red, white and blue Minis, and would help them in any way possible. But they were wrong: BMC wasn't in the least bit interested. BMC eventually sold them six Minis at trade cost, and the others (about 30), they had to buy at retail price. Caine was angry: 'What a dumb load of bastards they were. That's the problem with British industry, no foresight, no foresight, no foresight.'

Peter Collinson, who died aged just 44 in 1980, never saw his film earn the cult status it now enjoys. 'I've never known somebody more enthusiastic about directing a movie,' recalls Caine. The picture was made with a sequel in mind, but sadly the picture was not a success in its most important territory – America – and the idea was abandoned.

The Italian Job has continued to amuse generation after generation, and today its influence is obvious in the winning cocktail of larger-than-life characters and street-smart London dialogue appearing in a range of Brit flicks that followed. The result of Collinson's direction is a film loaded with Sixties swagger, swinging music, quotable lines and cars to die for. It's a movie that looks great, sounds great and truly stands the test of time.

THE ITALIAN JOB

The Battle of Britain

(1969)

World War II epic UK Colour 126 mins

Laurence Olivier, Robert Shaw, Christopher Plummer, Susannah York, Ian McShane, Michael Caine

Director: Guy Hamilton

Producer: Harry Saltzman and S Benjamin Fisz

Screenplay: James Kennaway and Wilfred Greatorex, from the book *The Narrow Margin* by Derek Wood and Derek Dempster

In this World War II epic, James Bond director Guy Hamilton created some amazing air battles and Blitz scenes, even if he didn't quite pull off the whole picture. The film gave a new meaning to the phrase 'star-studded'. Caine shared top billing with the likes of Laurence Olivier, Robert Shaw, Christopher Plummer and Ian McShane, no single actor dominating the film (although Olivier came close).

The $10 million film tells the story of Britain's greatest aerial battles and the non-stop action includes spectacular dogfight scenes. For authenticity, the production company acquired 100 genuine World War II aircraft; at the time producer Saltzman could boast proudly that he was in charge of the eleventh biggest air force in the world. Saltzman was keen to keep the flavour of the film British and, even before production began, turned down one financial backer because they asked for the story to be told from an American point of view.

The Battle of Britain was shot in Northweald Aerodrome in Essex and on the RAF bases at Duxford and Hawkinge, which the art department dressed up to look like World War II locations. The movie also used exterior locations at St Catherine's Dock, London and overseas in France and Spain. Despite the realism achieved in the locations and action sequences, the critics complained that the film lacked emotional content, the script allowing no time for the actors to invest any 'character' into their roles, which ultimately produced a film of spectacular aerial photography and little else.

Caine's performance, however, was good, even though he appeared in a minor role, as Squadron Leader Canfield. He spent the majority of the film shouting commands from behind the controls of a spitfire but made an early exit halfway through the movie when Canfield's spitfire descends into the ocean. His

> **He spent the majority of the film shouting commands from behind the controls of a spitfire**

fleeting appearance, but top billing, proved that by 1969 Caine was considered a major 'movie star'. Despite the cameo role, which required (in Caine's own words) '… not much effort on the acting front …', Caine felt it was a worthwhile project, if only for the experience of meeting the real life surviving pilots who were hired by the producers as technical advisors. The production team even enjoyed the expert advice of Adolf Galland, the Nazi pilot who had led the battle for the German side.

On Caine's last day, Guy Hamilton, the director, in his constant drive for realism, persuaded the reluctant star to taxi up the runway in the fighter plane. The technical advisor warned Caine not to touch the red button that rested next to his knee. 'What will it do?' asked Caine. 'You'll take off,' the advisor replied.

The Last Valley

(1971)

Historical drama UK Colour 119 mins

Michael Caine, Omar Sharif,
Florinda Bolkan, Nigel Davenport,
Per Oscarsson, Arthur O'Connell
Director/Producer: James Clevell
Screenplay: James Clevell, from
the novel by JB Pick

> "...if *The Last Valley* had been a smash hit what sort of direction would Caine's career have taken?"

The Last Valley, set in 1641, is a strange, ambitious, but fascinating historical epic, in which 17th-century German soldier Caine and scholar Sharif discover a peaceful, hidden European valley that has escaped the ravages of the Thirty Years War. Sharif's scholar persuades the Captain to spare the inhabitants any violence. As the two characters form a close friendship, the Captain is recalled to his army duties beyond the confines of the hidden valley, only to return there later to die.

Beautifully shot in Austria in 70mm, many critics hailed this as one of Michael Caine's finest films. But audiences just couldn't accept him in such an un-British role, especially after Alfie. 'I played a German in *The Last Valley* … But the image was so heavy that people wouldn't accept it,' he told William Hall. *The Last Valley*, was, however, a turning point in Caine's career: it was the first time he had earned half a million dollars for a film. Earning his money, he took the role very seriously; he cared deeply about the film, listening to English dialect records in order to devise a subtle Germanic accent.

As principle photography commenced, Michael had to overcome his worst fear: horse riding. His on-screen partner Sharif needed no encouragement to gallop at speed, and on one occasion Michael's horse bolted unexpectedly, and only when it stopped did Michael realize that it was the sword by his side slyly tapping the horse that was feeding the stallion instructions.

Caine was hurt by the public reaction to *The Last Valley*. 'It is a performance of which I'm particularly proud, one of the best performances I ever gave, as a matter of fact'. The prestigious film journal *Films and Filming* agreed and awarded him their Best Actor award in 1970. During production, Caine told a journalist from *The Sun*: 'I've no intention of just working for money. I won't do anything unless I'm passionate about it.' One wonders whether the public reaction to *The Last Valley* was responsible for his change of attitude, the reasoning behind his choice of the most lucrative but critically flawed roles in his later career. But as film journalist Anne Billson points out in her 1991 book, if *The Last Valley* had been a smash hit what sort of direction would Caine's career have taken? 'Would he have been cast in a lot of similar heavy-duty costume roles?' Would audiences have been denied *Educating Rita*, *Dirty Rotten Scoundrels* and *Hannah And Her Sisters*?

The Last Valley is rarely shown, and it remains an experience Caine would rather not talk about: a brave attempt for which he received very little recognition.

Get Carter

(1971)

Crime drama UK Colour 106 mins

Michael Caine, John Osborne,
Ian Hendry, Britt Ekland,
Brian Mosley

Director: Mike Hodges

Producer: Michael Klinger

Screenplay: Mike Hodges, from the
novel *Jack's Return Home* by Ted Lewis

Michael Caine entered the Seventies an icon, and with *Get Carter* he sealed his reputation as gangster number one in British cinema.

It was Michael's macho roles in *Alfie*, *The Italian Job* and *Get Carter* that created an iconic rebirth for Caine in Britain in the Nineties. 'If you look at Englishmen in films, they are either homosexual, bisexual, cold, repressed, fucked up, no good with women, bad lovers, kinky or insane. The Englishman in films has always been bad with women. Then here you have an actor as Alfie who went out and screwed them all, in *The Italian Job* he stole the gold and screwed them all, and in *Get Carter* he killed all the bad guys and screwed all the girls. So there you have three icons … which is me.'

Written and directed by Mike Hodges, *Get Carter* was based on Ted Lewis' novel *Jack's Return Home*. This terrific British thriller tells a tale of raw revenge within the terraces of Newcastle-upon-Tyne, and its impact is undiminished since it was first released in 1971. The movie became the genesis of the gangster genre, the film from which *Lock Stock* and *Snatch* et al were derived.

Michael Caine, together with producer Michael Klinger and director Mike Hodges, had formed the '3M company': Mike, Mike and Mike. *Get Carter* was their first project.

Caine had some knowledge of the dark underworld of gangsters. As he once said about his character, 'I modelled him on an actual hard case I once knew. I watched everything the man did. I even saw him once put someone in hospital for 18 months. Those guys are very polite, but they act right out of the blue. They're not conversationalists about violence, they're professionals.' Characters such as Jack Carter were pretty

> **If you look at Englishmen in films, they are either homosexual, bisexual, cold, repressed, fucked up, no good with women, bad lovers, kinky or insane**

common in the Elephant and Castle in London where Caine grew up. 'Carter was part of my childhood folklore.'

Caine was joined in the cast by playwright John Osborne, who played the central villain in the picture (Cyril Kinnear), although there was little opportunity for him to get to know Osborne as much as he would have liked: 'He seemed to be someone who didn't like many other people so I kept out of his way, in case I was one of them.' Britt Ekland is also part of the cast, although her role is minor. Her only memorable scene is the highly charged phone-sex scene in which Carter whispers erotically down the phone to a semi-dressed Britt writhing on the bed.

The film was financed by MGM, costing £750,000. Caine took the role for various reasons, most notably because he felt that up until that point he had always played nice people: 'Even Alfie

was nice in a way. This character was an utter brute.' Audiences were shocked by the movie's graphic violence but today the film looks significantly tame compared to recent gangster offerings. Caine claims the picture was made to shock its audiences: 'Every time somebody got hit we actually showed you

Carter was part of my childhood folklore

what happened ... that it hurts'. With *Get Carter*, Caine turned in a legendary performance, providing impersonators with a thousand punch lines. 'I think it's a brilliant movie by a brilliant director,' reflects Caine. 'It never lost any money, but it didn't make any.'

Kidnapped

(1971)

Adventure UK Colour 102 mins

Michael Caine, Trevor Howard, Jack Hawkins, Donald Pleasence, Gordon Jackson, Vivien Heilbron

Director: Delbert Mann

Producer: Frederick H Brogger

Screenplay: Jack Pulman, from the novels *Kidnapped* and *Catriona* by Robert Louis Stevenson

'It was an absolute disaster from beginning to end,' recalls Michael Caine, referring to *Kidnapped*, which was the second Robert Louis Stevenson adaptation in which he appeared (see *The Wrong Box*). *Kidnapped* was actually based on two of Stevenson's books, the other source being the sequel *Catriona*.

Adopting a Scottish accent, Caine went for a witty portrayal of the outlaw Alan Breck, holding together a film that one critic referred to as stiff porridge. The movie reunited him with veteran Jack Hawkins, now without a voice after losing it to cancer. The two had paired up seven years before in *Zulu*.

Kidnapped experienced a troubled production, running out of money halfway through the shoot. In fact Caine never even received his pay cheque – something he would never forget. 'I refuse to discuss it. I'm a professional, and if I don't get paid I don't talk about it.' He vividly remembers while shooting on the Isle of Mull, director Delbert Mann announcing an unexpected change to the shooting schedule. As the weather happened to be so nice, he ordered Caine to deliver two pages of dialogue at one-hour's notice. The experience taught Caine a valuable lesson: 'Learn your lines for the whole film before you start shooting.'

" It was an absolute disaster from beginning to end "

Sleuth

(1972)

Mystery UK Colour 138 mins

Laurence Olivier, Michael Caine,
Alec Cawthorne, Margo Channing,
John Matthews, Teddy Matthews
Director: Joseph L Mankiewicz
Producer: Morton Gottlieb
Screenplay: Anthony Shaffer, from
his play

Adapted by Anthony Shaffer from his own original play, and directed by Joseph L Mankiewicz, *Sleuth* provided Caine with arguably his most challenging role opposite the legendary Laurence Olivier. The action takes place in the country house of Andrew Wyken, a successful writer played by Olivier, who has invited Caine's character Milo Tindle to stay for the weekend. A jumped-up hairdresser, Tindle is having an affair with Wyken's wife Marguerite, played by Eve Channing.

A milestone in his career, Caine was both excited and nervous about appearing opposite such a polished actor: 'Olivier, by most standards, is the greatest actor in the world and here I was going into a two-handed piece with him, so it was awe-inspiring to say the least'. However, he need not have been so apprehensive: 'I did a scene on the stairs where he was supposed to shoot me and I did a hysterical cry thing, which was quite difficult to do. At the end he gave me the greatest compliment anyone has ever given me since I became a professional actor. He said to me "I thought I had an assistant, Michael … I see I have a partner".'

Caine was in awe not only of his co-star but also his director, Mankiewicz: 'He knows what you want to be achieving, and he also knows the moment you've got it.' The film was a tough shoot, with 14 intense weeks at Pinewood Studios on only a few interior sets. The 'old school' director pulled in production designer Ken Adam (of James Bond film set fame) to design an interesting interior. As Caine remembers, 'Ken Adam created a weird feeling with the interiors. It was real oak in the hallway not a load of plastic.'

Many have asked Caine what he learned from working so closely with one of the world's most gifted actors, but his reply remains the same: 'No … nothing specific, just how to take care of myself … He was one of those few people with whom it was a privilege to work, and an honour.' Both actors were nominated for an academy award, but lost out to Marlon Brando's performance in *The Godfather*. Brando didn't attend the ceremony, which annoyed Caine. 'Doesn't he owe that town anything? He should treat the Oscar with the respect it deserves.'

"I thought I had an assistant, Michael ... I see I have a partner"

Pulp

(1972)
Comedy thriller UK Colour 97 mins
Michael Caine, Mickey Rooney,
Lionel Stander, Lizabeth Scott,
Nadir Cassini
Director: Mike Hodges
Producer: Michael Klinger
Screenplay: Mike Hodges

A year after Mike Hodges, Michael Caine and Michael Klinger had finished work on *Get Carter* they began work on their second collaboration, *Pulp*.

An Englishman living in the Mediterranean makes a living from churning out pulp thrillers. Approached by a public relations officer, he is asked to write the biography of retired Hollywood star Preston Gilbert, who is soon assassinated. Caine's character, Chester Thomas King, discovers he is the next target, as Gilbert has supposedly spilled the beans to him on a past scandal.

The idea for *Pulp* emerged when Hodges first saw *Get Carter* on the big screen and was struck by the reaction to the film's violence. 'It made me want to make a film about why people want to go and see violence, and about the commercialisation of violence.' *Pulp* was almost a bookend to *Get Carter*, creating humour from the subject of violence.

Hodges relished the chance to make a second picture with Caine, following their previous collaboration: 'I had enjoyed working with Michael Caine and it had been a successful partnership so I was keen to work with him again.' As with *Get Carter*, Michael Caine was on producing duty with Klinger. They filled the cast with veteran Hollywood names such as Lizabeth Scott and Mickey Rooney. 'One of the things that fascinates me working in movies is the opportunity I occasionally get to work with stars familiar from my boyhood,' says Caine, specifically on working with Rooney.

" **...in a business where wallets are kept over the heart it did not count for much** "

It was originally planned that the film would be shot in Italy, but Hodges discovered that the Mafia dominated the majority of locations he wanted to use, so the shoot was moved to Malta. Caine disliked everything about the location. When one BBC reporter asked him what he thought was the best part of the island his answer was simple: 'the plane home'.

Many critics argued that *Pulp* was nowhere near as good as *Get Carter*. Hodges agreed: 'There are parts of *Pulp* I would like to have tightened up. But I think Michael is as excellent in it as he is in *Get Carter*. He played the character seedy and overweight and his voice-over is brilliant.' Caine had his own thoughts on the film, commenting in his autobiography, 'It was really an oddball of a movie that really never quite worked. Its heart was in the right place, but in a business where wallets are kept over the heart it did not count for much.'

The Black Windmill

(1974)

Spy thriller UK Colour 106 mins

Michael Caine, Joseph O'Conor, Donald Pleasence, John Vernon, Janet Suzman, Delphine Seyrig, Joss Ackland, Clive Revill

Director/Producer: Don Siegel
Screenplay: Leigh Vance, from the novel *Seven Days To A Killing* by Clive Egleton

Helmed by *Dirty Harry* director Don Siegel, *The Black Windmill* was labelled a disappointing affair by many critics, suggesting Siegel didn't quite have the ability to re-create a tale of British espionage as successfully as one of gangland America.

Caine plays Major John Tarrant, whose son is kidnapped by a mysterious military organization, which demands diamonds in return for his release. The plot becomes over complicated in places and thickened with double crosses and false identities, but these don't detract from the fine performances, most notably from Donald Pleasence.

Shot in London, Paris and the Sussex countryside, *The Black Windmill* was a remake of the Alfred Hitchcock film *The Man Who Knew Too Much*, which itself had also been remade 20 years earlier. Many felt this third attempt should never have been made. 'I did it to make a picture

with Don Siegel,' says Caine. 'I've always admired him, but every time I make a picture with a director I've admired it never works out right!'

Like *Dirty Harry* the film was tough and violent. It was intended for television but in the end was considered too brutal and was released theatrically. Caine agreed with the negative reviews but said, 'After Harry Palmer I thought I would never do another spy film. But the temptation of working with Siegel was enough to get me back into the Service.'

> **" I did it to make a picture with Don Siegel "**

The Marseilles Contract

(1974)

Thriller UK/Fr Colour 89 mins

Michael Caine, Anthony Quinn, James Mason, Maureen Kerwin, Marcel Bozzuffi, Catherine Rouvel, Maurice Ronet

Director: Robert Parrish
Producer: Judd Bernard
Screenplay: Judd Bernard, from his story *What Are Friends For?*

'I don't care what the script is like I'll do it,' said Caine when he heard *The Marseilles Contract* (or *The Destructors* as it was known in the States) was to be filmed in the south of France during the British winter. Producer Judd Bernard had even reportedly said to Caine, 'I won't send you the script because you will probably turn it down.' As Caine recalls in his memoirs: 'The picture turned out to be a flop, but I didn't care. We had a wonderful time … I always try to get my priorities right.'

Caine played John Deray, a professional lone assassin hired by the head of the Parisian arm of the American Narcotics Bureau to kill a drugs baron. The critics weren't convinced, nor were audiences. Only the presence of Anthony Quinn and James Mason, along with some eye-catching Paris and Marseilles locations adds any interest to the stereotypical characters and overly familiar plot. As Caine said of his co-stars: 'We're old friends. Both of them have marvellous confidence in their own ability … I love working with pros.'

The Marseilles Contract died the moment it was released, but Michael Caine wasn't bothered: he had had the time of his life down in Monaco with his mates. 'But Judd had been right about the script – it was never very good,' he confessed.

> **Judd had been right about the script – it was never very good**

The Romantic Englishwoman

(1975)

Comedy drama UK/Fr Colour 111mins

Glenda Jackson, Michael Caine,
Helmut Berger, Marcus Richardson,
Kate Nelligan, Rene Kolldehof,
Michael Lonsdale, Beatrice Romand,
Anna Steele, Nathalie Delon
Director: Joseph Losey
Producer: Daniel M. Angel
Screenplay: Tom Stoppard and Thomas
Wiseman from his novel

Many critics suggested that *The Romantic Englishwoman* was merely 'trash masquerading as art', even though it boasted such talent as British playwright Tom Stoppard and American director Joe Losey.

Caine portrays successful writer Lewis Fielding, who, while writing his latest screenplay, suspects his wife, Glenda Jackson, is having an affair with a drug courier, played by Helmut Berger. The courier eventually moves in with the couple and a complicated love story ensues. In fact the plot was so intricate that even Caine struggled to tell a *New York Times* reporter the nature of the film. 'I don't find it easy to describe. It's essentially a contemporary triangle', he mused. Some critics felt that the film, which is set mostly in Weybridge, Surrey, took itself far too seriously.

Caine's role was the complete antithesis of the many heroes he had portrayed in the early Seventies, which he relished, claiming: 'It attracted me because for the first time in my life I was playing someone who if I met him in real life I would not only dislike but despise.' He later claimed, 'There was nothing of myself I could bring to that role, so I had to construct the character from the ground up … It was pure performance.'

With *The Romantic Englishwoman* Caine broke a rule that he promised he never would: he appeared nude. He argues that one of the most important factors with acting on screen is the attention that the audience pays to eyes, claiming that a nude scene distracts that interest. However, Caine regularly mentions his enjoyment of starring opposite Glenda Jackson, considering her to be the best actress he has ever worked with. The feeling was mutual: 'I enjoy working with him because he gives so much back',

Jackson explains. When Jackson later became a Member of Parliament, Caine pondered in his memoirs: '… I have made love to an MP and a Socialist one at that. There's no business like show business!'

Caine claims this movie was his first and last foray into the world of art-house movies, but he felt the film helped his 'method acting'. In one particular scene his character had to shout at everyone around him, something Caine felt came easily to an improviser. Every little thing that could go wrong did go wrong on the morning before this scene was shot and irritations on set caused Caine to become bad-tempered, which he feels helped his performance on screen.

"There was nothing of myself I could bring to that role, so I had to construct the character from the ground up ... It was pure performance"

The Man Who Would Be King

(1975)

Adventure US Colour 123 mins

Sean Connery, Michael Caine,
Christopher Plummer, Saeed Jaffrey,
Karroum Ben Bouih

Director: John Huston

Producer: John Foreman

Screenplay: John Huston and
Gladys Hill, from a story by
Rudyard Kipling

The Man Who Would Be King
features one of the best on-screen
partnerships imaginable: Sean
Connery and Michael Caine. In
fact the film was destined for
success before the cameras even
started rolling because, as Caine
remarked, 'you had both James
Bond and Harry Palmer in the
same movie'.

The film centres on the
adventures of two disruptive ex-
army sergeants, Daniel Crovot
and Peachy Carnehan, played by
Connery and Caine respectively.
The officers are determined not to
return to England after their
service in India ends and instead
run riot across Afghanistan, gun-
running, blackmailing and
stealing, before attempting to
set themselves up as kings in
the foothills of the Himalayas.
Although the film can be enjoyed
as light-hearted entertainment,
the heart of the story is dark: one
of greed and the vanity of
human endeavour.

Director John Huston originally
cast Humphrey Bogart and Clark
Gable in the lead roles, but
following Bogart's death the
project was shelved. Other duos
were bandied about, including Paul
Newman and Robert Redford – an
attempt to re-create the success of
*Butch Cassidy and the Sundance
Kid* perhaps? Newman felt that
although the script was fantastic
the pair would be miscast as
Victorian Englishmen and
suggested to Huston the idea of
teaming up Connery and Caine. As
it turned out this pairing is a joy to
watch on screen, neither actor
trying to upstage the other.

**You sometimes
make a film
that you feel
may last after
you are dead
... I think this
will last**

As Caine recalls: 'I remember Sean and I used to choreograph things … we helped each other, we never tried to compete.' And later to journalist William Hall: 'I reckon it is the best relationship I have ever had with an actor.'

Despite his relaxed relationship with his co-star, Caine was in awe of his director, but remembers fondly the experience of working with him: 'John Huston didn't say much, but when he did you had better listen … My view of him is that if you ever heard God speak he would sound like John Huston.' Huston gave advice to Caine that he would remember long after the movie: 'Two days into shooting I was doing a very long speech and he said, "Cut". I said, "What's the matter, I didn't make a mistake?" "You can speak faster, Michael, he's an honest man." Ever since then when people speak slowly I think "Wait a minute … ." '

The Man Who Would Be King was a tough picture to shoot, filmed on location in Marrakech in Morocco, but was an enjoyable shoot for everyone. In his memoirs, Caine remembers it as: "… a very happy experience, due mainly to the friendship that developed between Huston, Foreman, Chris Plummer, Sean and myself. At the end of the shoot we knew that, even if we had been before, we were no longer "little men". Caine was even fortunate enough to work on location with his wife Shakira, who pops up in the movie as Danny's bride Roxanne. Although her appearance is fleeting, with only one scripted line, it was delivered in a spectacular wedding scene that took two days to shoot.

The film was another important milestone in Caine's career: not only was it a glorious success among a spate of disasters, but also it was his favourite performance of his career. 'You sometimes make a film that you feel may last after you are dead … I think this will last.'

" if you ever heard God speak he would sound like John Huston "

A Bridge Too Far

(1977)
World War II drama UK
Colour 168 mins
Dirk Bogarde, James Caan,
Michael Caine, Sean Connery,
Edward Fox, Elliott Gould,
Gene Hackman, Anthony Hopkins,
Hardy Kruger, Laurence Olivier,
Ryan O'Neal, Robert Redford,
Maximilian Schell
Director: Richard Attenborough
Producer: Joseph E Levine
Screenplay: William Goldman

Richard Attenborough's epic retelling of one of the biggest catastrophes of World War II is impressive enough, with its fabulous parachute jump sequences and stunning panavision cinematography, even without the huge cast list of Hollywood names. Surrounded by the talents of Olivier, Redford, Bogarde and Caan, Caine played Colonel Joe Vandeleur, Commander of the tank column, in this true story of the courageous but unsuccessful attack by British paratroopers on the bridge at Arnhem.

During the making of the film, producer Joseph E Levine said of his star-studded cast: 'These are not cameo roles. Every role played by these actors is a real part. We are not making a film in which a star actor pops up for two minutes so we can use his name above the title.'

Screenwriter William Goldman recalls that, with such an array of stars, the screenplay was a logistical nightmare to write. Who do you focus on? Who becomes the protagonist? Billed in alphabetical order, Caine's role was minimal, with just five days' filming in Holland. Says Caine: 'It was good money for very little work, but I did wonder at the time where the market for such an expensive film would be.'

Caine was, however, understandably on edge, as the Colonel on whom his character was based was on location for the entire shoot to aid Attenborough's crew and ensure the movie's authenticity. As Caine recalls in his autobiography, '... at the end of the first day I asked him [the Colonel] how he felt about the way I was playing him. "You are taller than I am and funnier", was his reply, so I guess he was satisfied.'

Attenborough was faithful to his team of actors: 'They aren't big star temperaments. You don't get to the top if you are unprofessional. You get there if you have real talent ... if you really have something going for you.' And Caine became fond of Attenborough, telling biographer William Hall, 'I've never seen a director with a firmer grip on what was happening. Richard told you every thought, where everyone was, what you were doing, why you looked like him.'

Although *A Bridge Too Far* is a breathtaking epic, the story suffers from too many plot strands, but Attenborough and his team have to be congratulated for undertaking a movie that needed the logistical planning of a real military operation.

> **... at the end of the first day I asked him [the Colonel] how he felt about the way I was playing him. "You are taller than I am and funnier", was his reply**

The Swarm

(1978)

Disaster US Colour 148 mins

Michael Caine, Katherine Ross,
Richard Widmark, Richard Chamberlain,
Olivia de Havilland, Fred MacMurray

Director/Producer: Irwin Allen

Screenplay: Stirling Silliphant, from the
novel by Arthur Herzog

'This was probably one of the worst pictures I ever made', admits Caine. *The Swarm* was the brainchild of producer/director Irwin Allen, who had made millions out of disaster movies *The Towering Inferno* and *The Poseidon Adventure*, but instead of flaming skyscrapers and sinking cruise liners, the disaster came in the form of killer bees and a bad script.

Having recently arrived in Hollywood, Caine was intrigued by the disaster movie and fancied dabbling in one himself. 'I did the movie because I wanted to do a disaster movie. I mean everyone else had done one, so why not me?' says Caine. 'And the subject really intrigued me. They're real bees, they really exist in the world … they're vicious bastards.' He was cast as entomologist Brad Crane at the centre of the story of a swarm of African killer bees moving west towards Houston, Texas, threatening the lives of thousands of Americans. Helping

Caine against the bees was a host of Hollywood stars, including Richard Widmark, Richard Chamberlain and Henry Fonda.

Caine was quoted after filming: 'It was one of the weirdest films I've ever been on – everyone going round in protective clothing and headgear, dressed in different colours so you could distinguish who they were! The director was in red. His assistants were in yellow, or orange. I was in white.'

'One of the more bizarre touches I'll always remember from this film, was the refrigerated trailer tucked away on one corner of the Burbank lot, with four ladies inside cutting off some of the stings from some of our bees,' recalls Caine. 'Actually it didn't harm them and it meant they could crawl all over us without hurting us. When you're spending fifteen million dollars on a picture, you can't afford to have the actors stung to death.' It wasn't just the occasional sting the cast had to

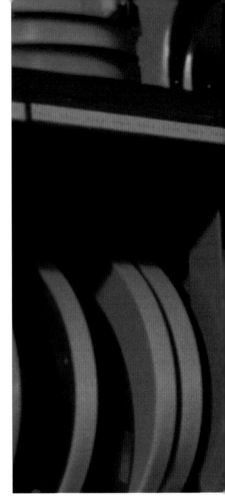

watch out for. What the bee experts hadn't told the cast was that bees never defecate within their own habitation, and always wait until they are away from the hive. Caine, Henry Fonda and Fred MacMurray all waited in their white smocks and as soon as Allen shouted 'Action!' the bees

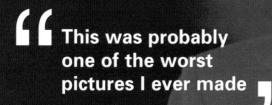

> **This was probably one of the worst pictures I ever made**

were released and swarmed towards the actors; within moments, and to the delight of the crew, the dazzling white of the actor's costumes gradually turned a peculiar shade of pale brown! The critics were unanimous in their dislike of *The Swarm*, *The Guardian* even suggesting: 'You could pass it all off as a sick joke, except that it cost $12 million, 22 million bees and several years out of someone's life.' But Caine admitted he quite enjoyed making the picture: 'I knew the script was a bit ropey, but I also knew that Irwin was the master of the disaster movie'. And Caine managed to take the sting out of the criticism, claming he had made the picture purely for money … enough to buy his family a new home in Beverly Hills.

California Suite

(1978)

Comedy US Colour 98 mins

Alan Alda, Michael Caine,
Bill Cosby, Jane Fonda,
Walter Matthau, Elaine May,
Richard Pryor, Maggie Smith
Director: Herbert Ross
Producer: Ray Stark
Screenplay: Neil Simon, from
his play

In 1978, after taking a terrible panning for *The Swarm*, Michael Caine made one of those films that showcased his talent as an actor and formed part of a group of pictures that is the 'Michael Caine legacy'.

Neil Simon adapted *California Suite* from his own successful stage play. The film is structured as four unconnected sketches with four different couples, but all exploring marriage, love and divorce. All the action takes place in the Beverly Hills Hotel and shows the vulgarity of Hollywood and the Los Angeles lifestyle.

Caine plays Sidney Cochran, an English antiques dealer who is visiting Los Angeles with his wife, celebrated (nominated for an Oscar) English stage actress Diana Barrie, played by Maggie Smith. The award goes to another actress and Barrie returns to her suite from the ceremony and hits the bottle. An argument ensues, with Cochran admitting he's bisexual.

Michael Caine had never before played a character of a different sexual persuasion on the big screen, but felt that: 'Being in show business I've been around a lot of bisexuals, so I didn't do any research at all'. He did, however, think about the character carefully, avoiding any stereotypical behaviour: 'What I did was to play the humanity of the person without the caricature.' As he told the *Daily Express*: 'I tried to get away from the "whoops dear" limp wrist, and show a man in some pain.' Although the critics loved Caine, the film really belonged to Maggie Smith. (In an ironic postscript, Smith won a real Oscar for her role in *California Suite*.)

The film helped repair some of the damage done to Caine's reputation with *The Swarm*.

> **What I did was to play the humanity of the person without the caricature**

Ashanti

(1979)

Adventure Swiss/US Colour 112 mins

Michael Caine, Peter Ustinov,
Beverley Johnson, Kabir Bedi,
Omar Sharif, Rex Harrison,
William Holden

Director: Richard Fleischer

Producer: Georges-Alain Vuille

Screenplay: Stephen Geller, from
the novel *Ebano* by Alberto Vasquez-
Figueroa

Immediately after setting up residence in America, Caine was keen to find a project to sink his teeth into …that project turned out to be a below-par adventure picture called *Ashanti*.

Michael Caine plays Dr David Linderby who is married to a fellow doctor (Beverly Johnson). The couple work in a small village in West Africa for the World Health Organization. As in adventure-movie tradition, things go disastrously wrong. A slave trader (Peter Ustinov) captures Johnson for a wealthy prince portrayed by Omar Sharif.

Ashanti was a tough shoot, the majority of the picture being filmed in the Sinai Desert. Unsurprisingly the location was extremely hot and Caine says it was the hardest film he has ever made: 'I loathed every second of it. I felt rotten all the way through.' After only one week of shooting in Kenya Caine was asked to pack his bags and return home while some minor changes were made. On his return Caine learned that those minor changes turned out to be the removal of both the director and the original leading lady.

The new director, Richard Fleischer, explained to film writer Michael Freedland that: 'It was just a waste of my time … One of the reasons why I'm glad I made the film, was because I worked with Michael.' The locations that had been selected by the sacked director were absolute murder, and took their toll on both the cast and crew. They were shooting in Africa during the rainy season, and Israel during the summer with temperatures reaching as high as 130 degrees.

When asked why he had made such an appalling piece of cinema Caine played his usual card: 'I did it solely for the money'. But by Caine's own standards it wasn't worth it: 'I have never been so unhappy in my career. I swore I would never do it again, no matter how broke I was.'

" I loathed every second of it. I felt rotten all the way through "

Beyond The Poseidon Adventure

(1979)

Drama US Colour 109 mins

Michael Caine, Sally Field, Telly Savalas,
Peter Boyle, Jack Warden,
Shirley Knight, Shirley Jones,
Karl Malden, Veronica Hamel,
Slim Pickens, Mark Harmon

Director/Producer: Irwin Allen

Screenplay: Nelson Gidding, from
the novel by Paul Gallico

Perhaps Caine decided he wanted a new patio to add to the house he had built on the proceeds of *The Swarm*. It became clear that he hadn't learnt his lesson when, in the same year, he readily signed on the dotted line for yet another of Allen's disastrous disaster movies. These films were at the beginning of the craze for big Hollywood special-effects movies, and Caine accepted roles in both *Beyond The Poseidon Adventure* and *The Swarm* to be a part of this new wave of movie-making. But he admitted that: 'Trying to make something of the rather cardboard characters in those movies is quite difficult.'

In *Beyond The Poseidon Adventure* Caine is joined by Sally Field and Karl Malden as a member of a salvage team sent to rescue the sunken *Poseidon* passenger liner. The team soon has to battle with the villain Telly Savalas, who is searching for the ship's valuable cargo. For Caine it was a demanding role; he even had to learn to scuba dive before shooting began. Special effects were regularly going wrong, and he later said that he was nearly killed twice during the making of the film.

The ship's hull was built on barges and sent floating in the Pacific, just off the coast of Malibu. Caine quaked at the diving sequences filmed in the freezing waters, telling journalist William Hall: 'Having always suffered from claustrophobia I didn't think I would be able to do it. But in this business you learn fast'. He described the movie as the Hollywood version of a 'snuff' movie: it was a film in which the actor really had to work hard for his pay cheque.

Looking back on the experience Caine is sceptical of Irwin Allen's directing ability: 'Irwin had decided to direct – his second attempt, *The Swarm* being his first. While I loved Irwin, and he was a great producer, a director he certainly wasn't.'

> **Trying to make something of the rather cardboard characters in those movies is quite difficult**

The Island

(1980)

Adventure US Colour 108 mins

Michael Caine, David Warner,
Angela McGregor, Frank Middlemass,
Don Henderson, Jeffery Frank,
Dudley Sutton, Colin Jeavons
Director: Michael Ritchie
Producer: Richard Zanuck and
David Brown
Screenplay: Peter Benchley, from
his novel

From the producers and writer of
Jaws came this disappointing film
of 17th-century pirates caught in
the Bermuda triangle.

Michael Caine has always been
known for the range of activities
in which he'll immerse himself to
make his performances as
authentic as possible, but this
time he had his reservations. On
arrival at the Antigua location,
Caine refused to get into the
water after hearing reports that
sharks were lurking nearby. 'I'm
not about to be the first movie
star to be eaten by a shark,' he
complained holding up the
production for hours until he was
definitely sure there was nothing
unfriendly in the water.

Universal originally wanted an
American actor to play the role
that was eventually given to
Caine. 'But strangely enough,' said
Caine, 'Peter Benchley who wrote
The Island about himself, always
had me in mind to play it.' The
studio was dissuaded from the

likes of Eastwood and Redwood
after the director and producers
Richard Zanuck and David Brown
all requested Caine. 'At any rate,'
the English actor joked, 'I'm a lot
cheaper than any of those other
guys.' He did say, however, 'I
heard that one of the reasons I got
The Island was that an executive's
wife had seen me in *The Swarm*
and had told her husband "This
man has carried that picture all on
his own. If he can carry that, then
he can carry this".'

During production, Caine stressed
the difficulty of creating a story
that an audience can believe in:
'This is a modern pirate story, and
when the pirates appear, the
situation becomes very delicate.
It's my job to control what the
audience thinks about the pirates
... And once you lose them, once
they suspend belief or decide
things look foolish, it takes twenty
minutes to get them back.'

The film was not well received
and many critics were starting to

question Caine's future as he
entered the Eighties. But at the
time he didn't seem too bothered,
commenting: 'I'm very well paid
and I'm not worried. I seem to
have the capacity for survival,
which, although I didn't know it
when I came into this business, is
now the most important quality.'

Looking back on the film in his
memoirs, Caine recalls that,
'Although the sharks didn't get us,
the critics did.'

> " I'm not about to be the first movie star to be eaten by a shark "

Dressed To Kill

(1980)

Thriller US Colour 100 mins

Michael Caine, Angie Dickinson, Nancy Allen, Keith Gordon, Dennis Franz

Director: Brian De Palma

Producer: George Litto

Screenplay: Brian De Palma

> **Now I could walk round Hollywood with my head held high once more**

Dressed To Kill was not only the movie Michael Caine was looking for, it was also the movie he needed to revive his flagging career following the string of disastrously bad pictures, including *Ashanti* and *The Swarm*. As he put it in his autobiography: '… there I was sitting in Hollywood with four clunkers in a row. I needed a miracle'.

In *Dressed To Kill* sex-starved housewife Angie Dickinson is murdered with a razor in a lift. Her son, played by Keith Gordon, and a prostitute (Nancy Allen) join forces to track down her killer. Caine completes the equation playing the victim's psychoanalyst, who turns out not only to be the murderer but also a transvestite. The idea of playing a transvestite murderer didn't appeal to many A-list actors and it is reported that many big American stars turned down the role for fear that it would damage their image. Indeed, when Brian De Palma first approached Caine with the idea the actor was obviously dubious; a picture of this nature was a big gamble for Caine: 'I'd never done that kind of real heavy thriller before'. Never mind a transvestite.

The gamble paid off and Caine is proud of the picture but is quick to admit that it was difficult to make and that working with De Palma was tiring: 'De Palma is a very exacting man, like a bloody surgeon, he goes on forever.' The scene in which the camera revolves 360 degrees as Caine greets a psychiatrist coming down the stairs took 26 takes. Caine complained that if he got the dialogue right, the camera was wrong and vice versa. 'It went on all morning and all afternoon,' he grumbled.

Dressed To Kill did good business at the box office and was Caine's biggest success since he'd arrived in the States. The critics also admired the picture, praising in particular its flashy effects and clever red herrings. De Palma was one of those filmmakers who grew up watching the old movies and packed their own films with 'tip of the hat' references to the great movie directors like Alfred Hitchcock. It did cause a stir in Bradford, where the Yorkshire Ripper was on the loose, and subsequently had to be withdrawn. There was only one major murder sequence in the entire film, but De Palma ensured the scene looked as bloody as possible in the hope it would last in people's memories, and would infuse fear for the remainder of the film.

Caine was relieved that the picture went down so well: 'Now I could walk round Hollywood with my head held high once more'.

Escape To Victory

(1981)

World War II drama US

Colour 111mins

Sylvester Stallone, Michael Caine, Pele, Bobby Moore, Osvaldo Ardiles, Paul Van Himst, Kazimierz Deyna, Hallvar Thorensen, Mike Summerbee, Co Prins, Russell Osman, John Wark, Soren Linsted, Kevin O'Calloghan, Max von Sydow, Gary Waldhorn, Daniel Massey, Tim Pigott-Smith

Director: John Huston

Producer: Freddie Fields

Screenplay: Evan Jones and Yabo Yablonsky

With *Escape To Victory*, producer Freddie Fields enlisted the talent of not only a handful of A-list movie stars, but also a squad of international football players and one of the most admired directors of all time, John Huston. Set in a German POW camp in 1943, it is the story of the German General High Command's propaganda football match between a team of German internationals and a group of British POWs, in front of a stadium packed with French occupants.

Michael Caine (then aged 50) convincingly kicked a ball around the pitch like David Beckman as he portrayed Captain John Colby, alongside football legends Bobby Moore, Pele, Mike Summerbee, and movie stars Sylvester Stallone and Max Von Sydow. Caine, as always, prepared for his role, studying footballers and the way they lived: 'I spent a great deal of time walking around [with footballers], sitting on my own, just seeing how they behave.' He

also took full advantage of the company of professional players, with Brazilian player Pele even coaching him on how to kick the ball properly. Caine told Pele: 'If you don't look after me during the football scenes, I won't look after you during the acting.'

Escape To Victory was shot in Budapest because it has the only stadium in Europe without floodlights. Caine and the rest of the cast found their 12-week stay in Hungary particularly depressing, but it was an ideal location. Not only was the labour

was over. Everyone went home but found themselves returning to Budapest several weeks later to shoot just one scene.

The movie saw Caine reunited with his old friend John Huston (they had worked together on *The Man Who Would be King*). As Huston remembers: 'Michael was exactly right for the part. He was the limey we wanted: smart and resourceful. I had enormous admiration for him, and I chose him for the role personally. I didn't have to give him any instruction … he knew more about the game than I did.' Huston allowed Caine to show his full potential. In the scene in which the prisoners discuss the possibility of escape, Michael rewrote his dialogue almost as the cameras rolled. 'What he actually said was far better than anyone could have written it', admitted Huston later.

Caine enjoyed his experience. Working with Sly Stallone, who by the early Eighties had become

familiar to audiences through the *Rocky* films, was not a problem for Caine and Stallone found Caine's less intense acting method refreshing: 'He doesn't deplete himself like so many actors do by staying in character all day long … when his scene is over, he'll flop back in his chair and laugh and joke with you.'

If you don't look after me during the football scenes, I won't look after you during the acting

cheap, but also the country was fairly undeveloped, making it visually suitable for a World War II prison flick. As the shoot came to an end, the actors' strike of 1980 was called. But there was still one scene to be shot. The film ceased production until the strike

The Hand

(1981)

Horror US BW and Colour 99 mins

Michael Caine, Andrea Marcovicci,
Annie McEnroe, Bruce McGill,
Viveca Lindfors, Rosemary Murphy,
Mara Hobel

Director: Oliver Stone

Producer: Edward R. Pressman

Screenplay: Oliver Stone, from the
novel *The Lizard's Tale* by Marc Brandel

Made by then Hollywood newcomer Oliver Stone, *The Hand* was the director's second movie. Borrowing heavily from Peter Lorre's 1946 horror film *The Beast With Five Fingers*, it told the story of cartoonist Jon Lansdale (Michael Caine) who loses his hand in a freak car accident, with the severed limb seeking violent revenge on all his enemies. Stone's multi-dimensional script explores the many facets of madness thoughtfully, and has been described as the 'thinking man's horror film', with Caine's possible insanity shown through distorted camera angles and clever flashbacks.

Caine took the film quite simply because it was a horror picture and he'd never tried that genre before, but later admitted he didn't enjoy making horror films and didn't want to do another one. Although Caine took the role seriously, visiting a physicist who had lost his hand in an experiment simply to see how he coped, the critics hated the film. As Caine records in his memoirs, '… although it was well made, I suppose it was just too weird to gain acceptance, and it was not a success even as a cult film.'

Even if the film didn't do anything for his career, he certainly gained one helpful tip from the affair, as he explained to journalist William Hall: 'The man loses his hand when he puts it out of the car window to signal, and a truck takes it off. Ever since then I never put my hand out of the window of a car …'.

"…the thinking man's horror movie"

Deathtrap

(1982)

Thriller US Colour 111 mins

Michael Caine, Christopher Reeve,
Dyan Cannon, Irene Worth, Henry Jones

Director: Sidney Lumet

Producer: Burt Harris

Screenplay: Jay Presson Allen, from
the play by Ira Levin

> ## I'd never kissed a man before, not even my father

Directed by Sidney Lumet, *Deathtrap* worked perfectly well on stage, but didn't cast the same spell when transferred to the big screen, even though Lumet used many long shots to give the piece a theatrical feel: 'He is one of the few directors who can make a film look interesting doing this,' says Michael Caine.

Deathtrap, like *Sleuth*, relied heavily on the skill of the two leads, this time in the form of Michael Caine and Christopher Reeve of *Superman* fame. Although it had a slightly bigger cast than *Sleuth*, at heart it was still a two-hander, taking place on a single set. This time Caine took on the Olivier role and Reeve played the young protégé. Jay Presson Allen wrote the screenplay and did not share the director's confidence that Caine was the perfect choice. Sue Mengers, Caine's agent, knew he was ideal, and she played a vital role in convincing the writer. 'I believed it was his next *Sleuth*,' she said.

The script demanded Caine and Reeve kiss, something that worried both actors. Caine was keen to skirt around the homosexual issue but Lumet insisted they show it. Recalls Caine: '… I'd never kissed a man before, not even my father … especially not on the lips.' He later admitted that: 'Christopher and I shared a bottle of brandy before we did that scene. We were both half drunk when we did that shot, but we did it perfectly because we only wanted to do one take.' The British tabloids, naturally, milked the story: 'My cissy screen smacker by Caine', screamed *The Sun*.

The American audience wasn't convinced by the picture, Caine feeling that it was '… too sophisticated for a mass American audience'. Although the film only did moderate business, the critics liked it, and it was another of those roles that enhanced Caine's reputation. Dyan Cannon, who appeared as Caine's wife in the film, insists: 'What Michael brings is a sense of complete believability. If what you are getting is real and powerful it allows you to be all of what you can be. You don't hold back.' During production many felt his performance was so strong that he was a contender for the Oscar. He didn't even get nominated.

After the film's release, Caine concluded that 'two guys kissing each other didn't do us any good'.

Educating Rita

(1983)

Comedy drama UK Colour 106 mins

Michael Caine, Julie Walters,
Michael Williams, Maureen Lipman,
Jeananne Crowley, Malcolm Douglas,
Godfrey Quiley
Director: Lewis Gilbert
Producer: Lewis Gilbert
Screenplay: Willy Russell, from his play

Educating Rita is, quite simply, a joy from beginning to end. It was also the film that Michael Caine's career needed, after a string of either commercial or critical failures towards the end of the Seventies. Directed by Lewis Gilbert, the film was based on Willy Russell's stage play of the same name.

Educating Rita is the sad but ultimately uplifting, not to say redeeming, story of Frank Bryant, an alcoholic English professor with a failing marriage, who comes across a young working-class hairdresser with a will to learn the finer points of English literature. In return she encourages and helps him put his life back on track. 'I saw it with an under-theme of an ugly professor who has an unrequited love for an attractive student', said Caine, who jumped at the role the moment Lewis Gilbert offered it to him.

Although the inspirational comedy is set in Liverpool it was actually shot in Ireland. Caine distinctly recalls shooting at Trinity College, Dublin. 'I remember the first day. I'd put on a lot of weight, I had a big beard, and I saw this bloke in a shabby old coat with a big stomach carrying a case of red wine. I said to one of the guys there "Does he look like

> **I saw it with an under-theme of an ugly professor who has an unrequited love for an attractive student**

me?" He said "That's the English Professor". I thought "I've got it! I've got it!" ' Michael Caine claims he modelled Frank Bryant on his business partner Peter Langan and playwright Robert Bolt.

Bryant was a drunk, and playing an alcoholic presented Caine with a challenge. Gilbert said to him shortly before rolling the camera, 'You're an actor who's trying to walk crooked and speak in a slurred voice … a drunk is a man who's trying to walk straight and speak properly.'

Originally Columbia wanted Dolly Parton for the main female role, but Gilbert was determined to cast Walters who had played the role on stage. *Educating Rita* was Julie Walters' first film. 'Michael was so kind to me in my first role. He hadn't forgotten what it was like to do your first part, he was really sensitive.' But Caine was so impressed by Walters' talent, that he said to Gilbert, 'My God, I've really got to start trying to act here … because this girl will act me right off the screen.'

Educating Rita reminded the critics and public alike just how good Michael Caine really is. He was nominated for an Oscar although he lost out for the third time to Robert Duvall for *Tender Mercies*. However, the consolation prize came in the form a BAFTA award for what is undeniably one of the best performances of his career.

The Honorary Consul

(1983)

Spy thriller 1965 UK Colour 102 mins

Michael Caine, Richard Gere,

Bob Hoskins, Elpidia Carrillo,

Joaquim de Almeida, A Martinez,

Stephanie Cotsirilos, Domingo Ambriz,

Eric Valdez, Nicholas Jasso,

Geoffrey Palmer

Director: John Mackenzie

Producer: Norma Heyman

Screenplay: Christopher Hampton, from the novel by Graham Greene

The Honorary Consul was the first of two movies adapted from the works of novelist Graham Greene, in which Michael Caine would appear. Here he plays an alcoholic British consul in a corrupt South American backwater, who's mistakenly kidnapped only to find that nobody wants to raise the ransom for his return.

Joining Caine fresh from his success in *An Officer And A Gentlemen* was sex symbol Richard Gere, portraying a doctor looking for his missing father, and British favourite Bob Hoskins, playing a morally ambiguous police chief. Gere reportedly told Caine during filming that it had been due to Caine's influence that he had decided on an acting career.

The critics were more than kind, stating that Caine's performance was outstanding, adding a much-needed burst of humour to the movie. But when Caine met Graham Greene in the mid-Eighties, several years after the film was released, he was nonplussed by the author's reaction. 'He started to tell me in no uncertain terms how much he disliked the film *The Honorary Consul*, but then he changed his tune and said he liked me in it, although I did not know whether he was telling the truth at this point.'

> **He [Graham Greene] started to tell me in no uncertain terms how much he disliked the film**

Blame
It On Rio

(1984)

Comedy US Colour 95 mins

Michael Caine, Joseph Bologna,
Valerie Harper, Michelle Johnson,
Demi Moore, Jose Lewgoy,
Lupe Gigliotti, Michael Menaugh

Director: Stanley Donen

Producer: Stanley Donen

Screenplay: Charlie Peters and
Larry Gelbart, from the film *Un Moment
d'Egarement* by Claude Berri

Directed by the legendary Stanley
Donen, (*Singin' In The Rain*,
Charade, *The Grass In Greener*)
Blame It On Rio sees Caine as
Matthew Hollis, a middle-aged
businessman taking a holiday in
Rio, who becomes romantically
involved with a teenager. The film
was considered risqué, but
everyone involved, including
Caine, thought they could get
away with it.

The film was based on the 1977
French picture *Un Moment
d'Egarement*. Flying away on
holiday to Rio de Janeiro with
business partner Victor, Matthew
Hollis's wife announces at the last
minute she will be spending her
vacation elsewhere. Teenage
daughters Nicole (Hollis'
daughter) and Jennifer join their
fathers. But without the
chaperone of a mother figure
Jennifer is soon frolicking with
Hollis on the golden sands.

Michelle Johnson plays Jennifer,
with newcomer Demi Moore as

Hollis' daughter Nicole. Years later Caine said of Moore: 'We did a pretty intense scene, and at the end of her close-up I said, "Demi, I think you will be a big star one day." And she said to me "Michael, you're full of shit".'

Originally called *Only in Rio*, the movie was shot over a 14-week period in Brazil on a $10 million budget. The story was initially set in the south of France, but the producers felt that audiences were becoming tired of the usual shots of Monte Carlo and Monaco and decided to reset the production in Brazil. 'It is almost a tourist movie of Brazil,' joked Caine during production. 'It is such a marvellous location.' He thought audiences would leave the cinema, '… laughing, having visited a beautiful country which you will want to visit yourself.'

The location was, however, the cause of some discomfort for Caine, who celebrated his 50th birthday in agony. On the first day of shooting Caine was required to chase co-star Michelle Johnson up the beach at night. No sooner had the cameras begun rolling than Caine tripped and broke his little toe.

Michael, you're full of shit

But the backdrop of Brazil did not tempt the critics. *Blame It On Rio* was condemned by reviewers for being nothing more than a scenic tour of a romantic destination. Some were shocked by the film's nudity. And some found unsavoury the age gap between Michael Caine's character and that of his female co-star, who was only 18. But Caine was quick to defend his involvement: 'I did it in order to prove I could do comedy … and with the reviews I got for it, I proved I could do comedy.' And as he later records in his autobiography, 'I am glad to say that the film went on to make a lot of money all over the world, despite all the fuss.'

Hannah And Her Sisters

(1986)

Comedy drama US Colour 102 mins

Woody Allen, Michael Caine,

Mia Farrow, Carrie Fisher,

Barbara Hershey, Max Von Sydow,

Diane Wiest, Lloyd Nolan

Director: Woody Allen

Producer: Robert Greenhut

Screenplay: Woody Allen

Like *Educating Rita*, Woody Allen's *Hannah And Her Sisters* gave Michael Caine a new lease of life. It was the movie that would win him the Academy Award he had always wanted. Although it was for Best Supporting Actor it was still an Oscar.

Like many of Allen's previous movies *Hannah And Her Sisters* has the director's beloved New York and downtown Manhattan as the backdrop. Caine starred opposite Allen's long-term partner Mia Farrow, playing her husband, a financial advisor who develops a passion for his wife's sister. The film explores the interweaving affairs of one family, particularly the three sisters (Mia Farrow, Barbara Hershey and Diane Wiest).

Caine found himself filming one particular love scene with Mia Farrow in her own bed, in her own Manhattan apartment with her husband behind the camera, and her ex-husband on a set visit.

It was a situation he was said to have found rather uncomfortable. But Caine reportedly found it easy working on a Woody Allen film. Farrow's mother was played by her real-life mother and Mia's children also appeared in the picture. Caine said Mia would often be found cooking her offspring a meal in the kitchen while Allen was setting up a shot in the living room.

One of the reasons he took the part was simply to work with Woody, sacrificing half his usual money in the process. 'Woody gives you more freedom to do as you like, possibly more than any other director that I've worked with, he was the complete opposite of what I thought he would be.' When they were discussing the character, Caine asked Allen if he could wear glasses. 'Of course, but why?' responded Allen. 'Because I figure I'm playing you in it,' he said. As Caine fondly remembers: '*Hannah And Her*

Sisters was Woody's warmest film … and the warmth came out in me.'

'I was surprised when I got the Academy Award for *Hannah And Her Sisters*. I had been nominated three times before, once for *Alfie*, once for *Sleuth* and once for *Educating Rita*. I really thought I would get it for *Educating Rita* but I didn't. When I got it for *Hannah And Her Sisters* it didn't even occur to me … I was astonished when I was even nominated.' He missed the Oscar ceremony as he was contractually tied to *Jaws: The Revenge*, which was shooting in the Bahamas. But with the golden statuette firmly in his hand Caine said '*Hannah and Her Sisters* proved to be the most unique of all films – one that was enjoyable to make and an artistic and commercial success.'

"
Hannah and Her Sisters proved to be the most unique of all films – one that was enjoyable to make and an artistic and commercial success
"

Mona Lisa

(1986)

Crime drama UK Colour 99 mins

Bob Hoskins, Cathy Tyson,
Michael Caine, Robbie Coltrane,
Clarke Peters, Kate Hardie,
Zoe Nathenson, Sammi Davis,
Rod Bedall, Joe Brown
Director: Neil Jordon
Producer: Patrick Cassavetti
and Stephen Woolley
Screenplay: Neil Jordan
and David Leland

In this chilling London-based thriller a gangster's chauffer, played by Bob Hoskins, falls for Cathy Tyson's troubled prostitute. Caine played the intimidating character Mortwell, the central 'bad guy'.

Hoskins recalls: 'They wanted Michael for the big villain, but we didn't have any money. I wouldn't have dreamt of asking him, it would have been like asking him the biggest favour going. But having him in it would have taken it to another level. He tormented the life out of me. He said, "I've had this script, *Mona Lisa*, you're in it, aren't you?" I was dying to say "Please, Michael, do it." We turned up on the first day and he said, "Hello son, didn't expect me to be here, did you?"'

Caine joked: 'I did it because Bob Hoskins is my mate, and because I think Neil Jordan will be one of the big directors of the future. I want to get in well with him before he's too famous so he'll give me a job when I'm old." In fact, Jordan directed with flair and zest creating an exceptional thriller.

The year of production was the year that AIDS fears were at their height, and they affected Caine like many others. One scene, in which he was required to visit a bathhouse, was filmed at The Sanctuary, one of London's top health clubs. Caine said at the time, 'Suddenly, I'm in the pool with eight naked guys and I kept thinking, "Am I going to get AIDS?" When they said "Put your head under and wet your hair", I got water from the tap and poured it over.'

The shoot was an emotional journey for Caine. As he wandered about the decaying Dickensian warehouses in South London on his first day of shooting, he finally arrived at a depressing Victorian building, which was now housing Bob Hoskins' production office. Caine asked what the building had been used for and Hoskins told him it was a hospital called Saint

"everything in acting in a sense is memory"

Olave's. Caine had heard that name all his life: it was the hospital in which he was born.

Mona Lisa gave Caine another chance to explore the dark gangster underworld that he had first encountered 15 years earlier in *Get Carter*. 'I am the gentlest person you could possible ever meet. But in *Mona Lisa* I played an extremely brutal and sadistic gangster. That just comes from

observation of where I grew up … everything in acting in a sense is memory.' Despite his role as a gangster in earlier films, he felt his role as Mortell in *Mona Lisa* broke new ground: 'It's the first time I've played a completely evil, unsympathetic character. It's a great deal of fun for me to play someone who is an absolute frightening creep.'

"I want to get in well with him [Neil Jordan] before he's too famous so he'll give me a job when I'm old"

Jaws: The Revenge

(1987)

Action adventure US Colour 86 mins

Lorraine Gary, Lance Guest, Mario Van Pebbles, Karen Young, Michael Caine, Judith Barsi

Director: Joseph Sargent

Producer: Joseph Sargent

Screenplay: Michael de Guzman, from characters created by Peter Benchley

'I have never seen the film but by all accounts it was terrible, but I have seen the house it built … and it's terrific', said Caine triumphantly in defence of his involvement with *Jaws: The Revenge*.

The last in the *Jaws* series created by novelist Peter Benchley, this dreadful tale of the Great White gets personal, as the shark follows the Brody family to the Bahamas. The finale features Caine attacking the beast by aircraft. Caine plays Hoagie, a pilot in the Bahamas. He took the role for a handful of reasons: location shooting in the Bahamas, a fat pay cheque and the chance to make a film that his daughter's friends would be interested in watching.

Jaws: The Revenge lacked the suspense of Spielberg's original, the general consensus being that the story was completely implausible and the body count too low, making the picture a disappointment for lovers of the genre.

Caine stressed it was important to make big-budget movies such as *Jaws* in order to make the smaller art-house features which he enjoyed immensely. But he remembers the shoot with affection: '*Jaws: The Revenge* will go down in my memory as the time when I won an Oscar, paid for a house and had a great holiday. Not bad for a flop movie…right?'

I have never seen the film but by all accounts it was terrible

The Fourth Protocol

(1987)

Spy thriller UK Colour 113 mins

Michael Caine, Pierce Brosnan,
Joanna Cassidy, Ned Beatty,
Ray McAnally, Betsy Brantley,
Sean Chapman, Peter Cartwright,
Julian Glover, Michael Gough,
Rosy Clayton, David Conville
Director: John Mackenzie
Producer: Timothy Burrill
Screenplay: Frederick Forsyth and
Richard Burridge, from the novel by
Frederick Forsyth

After losing the first opportunity to become the new James Bond because of contractual problems with the TV series *Remington Steele*, Pierce Brosnan tried his hand at life on the other side of the wall, playing a dastardly Russian spy, out to blow up an American airbase in England. Michael Caine played the super agent out to stop him, in *The Fourth Protocol*, which is based on the Frederic Forsyth bestseller.

Caine also earned himself a co-producer's credit on the film, investing $705,000 of his own money into the $11.3 million production, with Forsyth investing a further $1.5 million. Many felt the film was too bland, too wordy. Caine himself agreed: '[It's] a talking picture not a moving picture,' he said. Caine, in fact, tried to persuade Forsyth, who was also adapting his own work, not to make the script as 'wordy' as the source novel. But as Caine rightly points out, it is very hard to get a writer to cut his own lines. 'I went there as the star and associate producer and one might have thought this would give me sufficient authority to put my own strongly held opinions into practice, but no chance.'

"...a talking picture not a moving picture "

With such a plot-heavy movie, *Variety* magazine suggested, perhaps rightly, that *The Fourth Protocol* may have worked rather better if it had been made as a mini-series.

Without A Clue

(1988)

Comedy Mystery UK Colour 101 mins

Michael Caine, Ben Kingsley,
Jeffery Jones, Lysette Anthony,
Paul Freeman, Nigel Davenport,
Paul Keen, Peter Cook, Tim Killick,
Matthew Savage, John Warner
Director: Thom Eberhardt
Producer: Marc Stirdivant
Screenplay: Gary Murphy and
Larry Strawther

Without A Clue saw Caine playing the world's most famous detective, Sherlock Holmes, although the twist in the plot reveals that he is nothing more than a figment of Dr Watson's imagination.

Ben Kingsley, who played Dr Watson, spoke to *Time Out* during the making of the picture about working with Caine: 'We work in very similar ways. Our Winnebagos are parked together, you can hear me pacing up and down doing my lines by myself, and he's doing exactly the same thing in his. Pacing up and down, working on rhythms, timings, inflections, working on his voice like a theatre actor.'

However bad some thought the movie was, Kingsley loved the experience: 'We rehearsed scenes with the crew and got a lot of laughs because we are a good double act.'

" Pacing up and down, working on rhythms, timings, inflections, working on his voice like a theatre actor "

Dirty Rotten Scoundrels

(1988)

Comedy US Colour 105 mins

Michael Caine, Steve Martin,
Glenne Headly, Anton Rogers,
Barbara Harris, Ian McDiarmid,
Dana Ivey

Director: Frank Oz

Producer: Bernard Williams

Screenplay: Dale Launer,
Stanley Shapiro and Paul Henning

Dirty Rotten Scoundrels remains Michael Caine's favourite comical performance to date. The picture was based loosely on the 1964 film *Bedtime Story*, which starred David Niven and Marlon Brando. Caine was, in fact, originally offered the movie several years earlier, under the title *The King Of The Mountain*, in which he was to star opposite one of the new crop of Eighties American actors known as the Brat Pack. Tom Cruise was suggested, but at the time he was a bit of a nobody and the producer couldn't find the financial backing.

When Steve Martin and director Frank Oz met with Caine and gave him the script to *Dirty Rotten Scoundrels*, he was interested in the role immediately. 'I was offered an absolutely marvellous part, in a comedy movie that despite some of my disastrous experiences in this genre looked absolutely foolproof.' The role is that of a veteran con man eking out a comfortable life on the French Riviera, who takes brash American Steve Martin under his wing. The two characters fall out when they compete over a rich heiress, who they both want to 'take to the cleaners'.

The contrast between the two leads is sheer magic: Martin plays his part with a crazy lunacy and Caine avoids the obvious laughs, playing the posh Brit to a tee. 'Steve is the most unselfish actor I have ever worked with … apart from Sean Connery,' said Caine, who understood it was important to play the role straight and to avoid competing with Steve Martin's crazy style. Caine's problem was how to react to this madness. He wisely chose the route that he has always taken with comedy in films: he played it straight, as though it was a mere drama, and allowed the humour to take care of itself.

Although the film was set in the south of France, Caine was aware that shooting there during the summer season would be a costly affair. He was waiting to be told that they would actually be filming somewhere like Yugoslavia, with shop front and road signs erected to give the location an authentic French feel. He was wrong. Director Frank Oz told him the whole production was to be based at the film studios in Nice. The location looked gorgeous on screen and it was. In fact, says Caine: '… it was the best location I have ever worked in.'

Writer Michael Freedman reported that when the film was first shown to the cast and crew, a great feeling of depression lingered over them, but audiences queued up in their millions to see Caine in his best movie since *Hannah And Her Sisters*. Caine admits it was Oz who was responsible for the movie's success, as noted in his memoirs: 'Frank Oz had turned out to be a master comedy director, very sympathetic towards all of us. So the work went well right from the start.'

"a comedy movie that...looked absolutely foolproof"

Bullseye!

(1990)

Comedy thriller US Colour 88 mins

Michael Caine, Roger Moore, Sally Kirkland, Deborah Moore, Lee Paterson, Mark Burns

Director/Producer: Michael Winner

Screenplay: Leslie Bricusse, Laurence Marks and Maurice Gran, from a story by Leslie Bricusse, Michael Winner and Nick Mead

Michael Winner's *Bullseye!* provided Michael Caine with the opportunity to team up with his old friend Roger Moore, who, for the past 15 years had been busy gallivanting around the globe as the third incarnation of Ian Fleming's superhero, James Bond. Many felt this dire attempt at comedy caper was just an excuse for the old pals to hook up together on screen.

The pair had been keen to find a project. Roger's agent then submitted the *Bullseye!* script, which writer Leslie Bricusse had written especially for them. 'It was rather like a glamorous *Carry On* film,' said Winner. 'It was immense fun to make as they're both tremendously nice people. Both Roger and I are a part of Michael Caine's very close circle of friends, and so there was quite a history between us all.'

Sidney Lipton (Caine) and Gerald Bradley Smith (Moore) are two con men out to steal a gem from under the noses of their look-a-likes who have made an amazing scientific discovery that will lead to cheap electricity. The duo set about selling the invention to the highest bidder, which leads them from London to Scotland before heading to the Caribbean. The scenes were all shot on location. The original screenplay called for principle photography to take place in Venice, but the financiers soon decided this was not possible.

The comedy owes its existence to *Gunga Din*, Rudyard Kipling's adventure of British soldiers and their dashing deeds during the native uprisings in 19th-century India. Producer Menahem Golan had teamed Moore and Caine in an attempt to recapture the magic of the 1939 version of that film, which starred Cary Grant and Douglas Fairbanks Jr. It never happened.

With a cast list of cameo performers, including John Cleese, Patsy Kensit and Jenny Seagrove, *Bullseye!* set new levels for critic vitriol. The film was appalling but the fun Caine and Moore seemed to have is visible on screen. As Caine told *Time Out*: 'We've been having a good old time, Roger and I!'

The film received a royal premiere but audiences weren't impressed. Recalls Winner: 'I think, perhaps, with Michael and Roger people expected something more important. It wasn't meant to be important, just fun!'

> **It was rather like a glamorous *Carry On* film**

Noises Off

(1992)
Comedy US Colour 99 mins
Carol Burnett, Michael Caine,
Christopher Reeve, Denholm Elliott,
Julie Hagerty, Marilu Henner
Director: Peter Bogdanovich
Producer: Frank Marshall
Screenplay: Marty Kaplan, from the
play by Michael Frayn

Caine had been taking a well-earned break when director Peter Bogdanovich telephoned to ask if he would like the role of a stage director in the movie version of *Noises Off*.

Adapted for the screen by Marty Kaplan, *Noises Off* focused on a group of American stage actors during the preparation for their pre-Broadway tour. Taking place entirely on one set, an English country mansion, the whole movie was shot on one soundstage at Universal Studios.

Caine was reunited with old friends, including Christopher Reeve. He joked that there was a clause written into their contracts that said they wouldn't have to kiss (see *Deathtrap*).

The chaotic scenes in this comedy belie the truth, as each scene was carefully choreographed. 'You can't ad-lib anything because it's all timing,' said Caine during filming.

Noises Off bombed. Caine was extremely disappointed 'We worked so hard to get it right but in spite of a magnificent cast and everybody going full blast, it seems that we never made it.'

He puts the film's failure down to the fact that audiences aren't interested in movies about actors, unless they are scandalous or tragic. He said in his autobiography 'They think we are spoiled, overpaid and lucky, which is true.'

**They think we [actors]
are spoiled, overpaid
and lucky, which is true**

The Muppet Christmas Carol

(1992)

Comedy drama US Colour 85 mins

Michael Caine, Steven Mackintosh, Meredith Braun, Robin Weaver, Donald Austin, Dave Goelz, Steve Whitmire, Jerry Nelson, David Rudman, Frank Oz
Director/Producer: Brian Henson
Screenplay: Jerry Juhl, from the novel *A Christmas Carol* by Charles Dickens

The one sure thing about Caine is that you never know what he's going to do next. In 1992 he provided his audiences with a Christmas treat as Ebenezer Scrooge. His leading lady? Miss Piggy. Surrounded by the likes of Kermit, the Cratchits and Gonzo, Caine hadn't been so good in years and visibly enjoyed the film as much as the audience.

The Muppet Christmas Carol was an interesting diversion for Caine, as not only was he playing opposite an entire cast of puppets, but also it was the first and (to date) the only family film he had made. He had now dabbled in almost every genre. The critics were generous too, with many picking up on Caine's wise attempt not to go for laughs. 'I'm not making any concessions to the fact I'm working with Muppets. The part wouldn't be as funny if I didn't play it straight and pretend they're human. And sometimes that means I have to act very

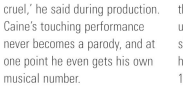

" It was an honour and a privilege to work with Miss Piggy. She's such a lovely swine "

cruel,' he said during production. Caine's touching performance never becomes a parody, and at one point he even gets his own musical number.

Caine confessed during the making of the picture that he'd '…always wanted to play with the Muppets. My daughter and I used to watch them on TV when she was young. We'd laugh and have a wonderful time. Now she's 19, and I hope she'll have the same reaction to this movie.' The role was a personal joy for Caine: 'All my friends worked on the TV *Muppet Show*, but that was only

a half-hour programme. I get to do a whole movie with the Muppets, so really … I win.'

Apart from working with the Muppets, another life-long wish for Caine was to take on a character from Dickens. 'This is a marvellous role. It's exciting for an actor to do a character like Scrooge who is very well written, very well drawn. I grew up in a very poor family.' Even though the story was told with Muppets, no attempt was made to water down the essence of the story, and the poignancy of the tale remains.

Asked by one journalist who his favourite Muppet was he replied: 'It was an honour and a privilege to work with Miss Piggy. She's such a lovely swine'.

Bullet To Beijing

(1995)

Spy thriller UK/Can/Rus

Colour 100 mins

Michael Caine, Jason Connery, Mia Sara, Michael Sarrazin, Michael Gambon, John Dunn Hill, Lev Prygunov, Burt Kwouk

Director: George Mihalka

Producer: Harry Alan Towers

Screenplay: Peter Welbeck, from the novel by Len Deighton

Midnight In St Petersburg

(1995)

Thriller UK/Can/Rus Colour 85 mins

Michael Caine, Jason Connery, Michael Sarrazin, Michael Gambon, Michele Rene Thomas, Tanya Jackson, Yuri Limonty, Michael Scherer, Gabriel Vorobyov, Lev Prygonuv, Olga Anokhina

Director: Doug Jackson

Producer: Harry Alan Towers

Screenplay: Peter Welbeck, from the novel by Len Deighton

In the early Nineties some bright spark had the daft idea of resurrecting Sixties icon Harry Palmer. The secret agent really should have stayed in his retirement home. Instead Caine was persuaded to don the horn-rimmed glasses again for two more adventures shot back to back.

It was producer Harry Alan Towers who set the ball rolling when he fell to pondering what happened to the out-of-work spies left over from the Cold War. After acquiring the necessary rights to both the novels and character, he personally wrote the screenplays under the alias Peter Welbeck.

In Welbeck's screenplays Palmer has retired from the British Secret Service and in the first movie, *Bullet To Beijing*, is working with the former KGB in Russia, trying to prevent North Korea from using biological weapons. Michael Gambon appears as a Russian magnate and Jason Connery as a Russian agent.

Midnight In St Petersburg has Palmer running a security firm in Moscow. When the girlfriend of one of his employees (Jason Connery) is kidnapped, Harry finds himself involved in an art fraud and the theft of a large quantity of plutonium.

The original idea was to shoot the first movie for a theatrical release and the second for cable broadcast in the States. Matthew Duda, senior vice president of program acquisitions and planning for the Showtime network, said 'It would be difficult to get Michael Caine to do an original TV movie. He's a well-established star who comes with a certain price. By having a theatrical locomotive we could make it work.' And Caine agreed: 'I did the TV movie because it was the only way they would make the feature'.

Bullet To Beijing and *Midnight In St Petersburg* were filmed over a 12-week period in Russia at a combined cost of $12 million. Disney was behind the distribution but pulled the plug on a theatrical release, so both titles went straight to video. Film writer William Hall reported that the official reason behind Disney's decision to abandon the films was that the executives thought Palmer was yesterday's man in the Nineties movie world of high-tech action and special effects. Producer Ed Simons said of the decision, 'Michael is understandably very angry. It's not a question of money – it's a matter of professional pride.'

Executives thought Palmer was yesterday's man in the Nineties movie world of high-tech action and special effects

Blood
And Wine

(1997)

Crime thriller US/UK/Fr

Colour 96 mins

Jack Nicholson, Stephen Dorff,
Jennifer Lopez, Judy Davis,
Michael Caine

Director: Bob Rafelson

Producer: Jeremy Thomas

Screenplay: Nick Villiers and Alison
Cross, from a story by Bob Rafelson
and Nick Villiers

Blood And Wine is a richly layered crime movie, which explores the lives and personalities of two dishonest lowlifes. The adult thriller, filled with dark twists, relies on the talent of its lead performers: Jack Nicholson and Michael Caine. The duo play a pair of immoral thieves who steal a costly necklace from a Florida wine dealer. In best movie tradition, the theft goes horribly wrong, highlighting the personal repercussions for men living on the edge of the law. Jennifer Lopez is thrown in to spice up the sexual content.

Nicholson was on board from an early stage; Caine was more of a last-minute casting decision, due to late changes being made to his character. 'We had made his character English,' said director Bob Rafelson. 'I thought, okay, Albert Finney, Ben Kingsley, this one, that one. Albert was busy, and Ben Kingsley wanted too much money, and somebody said, "Well, Michael Caine has heard about your movie, and

he'd like to work with you".' Rafelson had reportedly been a fan of Michael's, '… but I had felt over the years, that he was doing just too much work. And I wanted something very special from him, which I had seen on film in moments, like in *Mona Lisa*.' The veteran director coaxed a wonderful performance from Caine. 'He was more than ready to work,' reflects Rafelson. 'Anxious to work. Anxious to dig deep.'

Under Rafelson's direction, Caine creates his nastiest villain since *Mona Lisa*, a terminally ill, coughing chain smoker spitting up blood, capable of sudden violence. In one sequence he beats Jack Nicholson with a golf club. But for all that, the character inspires some sympathy from the audience; he is a man who has had a long and hard career as a thief, but has nothing to show for it. There is some hope for him as he lurks in Miami to pull off one final heist.

I wanted something very special from him

The film was an important personal project for Rafelson (he'd made *Easy Rider* and *Five Easy Pieces* with Nicholson), who had been developing it for several years. 'I worked on nothing but this,' he said after filming wrapped. 'Independent movies take a long time to get made when you're up in this bracket, which at the time was about £11 million. It's rare for independent companies to cover a movie like this.' The director also wanted to give the movie a particular mood: 'I shot *Blood and Wine* almost entirely in close-up. I wanted to get into the eyeballs of the characters. I like a certain theatricality.'

Blood And Wine is a smart, engrossing adult thriller with suspense but great personal stories, and Nicholson and Caine made a deliciously sleazy double act. The film became an important step in Michael Caine's climb back to the top.

Little Voice

(1998)

Comedy drama UK Colour 92 mins

Jane Horrocks, Brenda Blethyn,
Michael Caine, Ewan McGregor,
Philip Jackson, Annette Badland,
Jim Broadbent

Director: Mark Herman

Producer: Elizabeth Karlsen

Screenplay: Mark Herman, from the
play *The Rise and Fall of Little Voice* by
Jim Cartwright

> **There are few actors who can play a sleazy but likable rogue who turns nasty, and Michael is one of them**

'I've made a lot of crap and a lot of money so I can afford to be artistic now,' said Michael Caine as he picked up a Golden Globe award for his performance as Ray Say, a sleazy and spectacularly unsuccessful local talent agent in Mark Herman's *Little Voice*.

'I wasn't looking for a job, I was just looking for a script to do,' said Caine after the picture wrapped. 'My agent rang and said "Hey, there's a great villain part in *The Avengers*, with Ralph Fiennes and Uma Thurman", I said "Yes, fine, go for it." Next day she rang me and said "I'm afraid Sean's got it." Then the *Little Voice script* came from nowhere. So you see, there is a God!'

Based on the highly acclaimed London play, the story follows Mari, an aging, on-the prowl widow with verbal diarrhoea, and her reticent, reclusive daughter who barely ever speaks. Dubbed Little Voice, this unusual young woman is hiding a rare gift: she may not talk, but she can sing, capturing the legendary personas and voices of Judy Garland, Shirley Bassey and Marilyn Monroe.

Caine was attracted to the richness of his character, and the opportunity to play a part creep, part charmer: 'Ray is stupid, ruthless and selfish but he doesn't see himself as bad. He has all the accoutrements of a loser: the flashy jewellery, the flashy clothes, but everything is to make up for the fact he hasn't made it. Little Voice is his last chance.' Caine put on two stone for the role, and once filming was complete, lost the flab in six months. Director Mark Herman said during the production of the film, 'There are few actors who can play a sleazy but likable rogue who turns nasty, and Michael is one of them. He is also one of those actors who every now and then turns in a truly surprising and unforgettable performance and I think he does that here. Audiences haven't seen him like this in a long time.'

However, the star of the show was Jane Horrocks as Little Voice, a character she had also portrayed on stage. Caine recalls: 'The first time I saw Jane sing, my character Ray is supposed to be thinking "I'm gonna make a fortune, I'm gonna get out of this rotten town", and I was supposed to be happy. But I had tears in my eyes. I remember saying to Brenda Blethyn "It's rather corny, but it's the first time I've ever actually watched a star being born".'

Little Voice put Michael Caine back on the map. As film critic David Eimer noted, 'It would have been natural for Caine to slide into retirement … Now he is busier than ever. For the first time he is making back-to-back films, and they're the sort of worthy, high-profile, but low-budget projects that he once would have scorned in favour of a big payday and a few weeks on a glamorous location.'

The Cider House Rules

(1999)

Drama US Colour 125 mins

Tobey Maguire, Charlize Theron,
Michael Caine, Delroy Lindo, Paul Rudd,
Jane Alexander, Kathy Baker,
Kate Nelligan

Director: Lasse Hallstrom
Producer: Richard N. Gladstein
Screenplay: John Irving, from his novel

Surprisingly, given the length of his career, *The Cider House Rules* was only the second time that Caine portrayed an American on screen (the first being in *Hurry Sundown* in 1967). He was terrified and only agreed to play the role after voice-coaching sessions and approval from other Americans. He said after the film was released: 'It just comes out now, I'm not aware of it.'

Directed by Lasse Hallstrom, with a screenplay by John Irving, *The Cider House Rules* was a touching story of a Twenties New England orphanage and the unusual doctor who runs it. The movie has the classic structure of a young man's journey: leaving home, discovering love and finding his place in the world. That man is Homer Wells (Tobey Maguire of *Spiderman*), a child raised in the orphanage and mentored by the institute's doctor, Dr Larch (Michael Caine).

Caine immediately fell in love with the Dr Larch character. The doctor is a hugely compassionate man with great concern for his charges, but has a firm belief in abortion. He believes in the right to perform abortions in order to prevent unwanted and unloved children being brought into the world and perpetuating the need for his own orphanage. As Caine said in the *Sunday Times*, 'He is probably the nicest and gentlest person I have ever played.' You don't so much watch him, you feel him: his complex, thwarted emotions; his pain; his love. 'I don't believe in abortion, and I don't think all women who have abortions believe in them either. But they are a reality.'

The Cider House Rules presented Caine with the opportunity to stretch his acting abilities even further, something that appealed even this late on in his career: 'Everything that you could think of to do emotionally as an actor is there. The film has elements of comedy and tragedy, but it isn't really either of those things entirely because it is about life.'

Hallstrom believed that Caine was the perfect choice for the role: 'I think Michael brings a weight and significance to the part that makes him a credible and interesting choice to play the head of this orphanage, the father of this family of orphans. He also has a wonderful sense of humour, wit and intelligence that I think makes him a perfect Larch.'

Although a number of British critics complained that he couldn't quite grasp the American accent, Caine insisted: 'It can't have been that bad. I won the bloody Oscar, didn't I?' And he was given a standing ovation as he picked up the coveted award, the second Oscar of his career, at the Dorothy Chandler Pavilion in Los Angeles.

Everything that you could think of to do emotionally as an actor is there

Quills

(2000)
Comedy/Drama US/DE/UK
Colour 124mins
Michael Caine, Kate Winslet, Geoffrey
Rush, Joaquin Phoenix
Director: Philip Kaufman
Producer: Julia Chasman, Peter
Kaufman and Nick Wechsler
Screenplay: Doug Wright

With a triumphant Oscar win behind him, Michael Caine really could pick and choose the roles he wanted, and decided to follow up *The Cider House Rules* with *Quills*, in which he played a prudish doctor with a mission to tame sadist supremo, the Marquis De Sade.

Quills boldly explored the final days of Marquis De Sade as a blistering black comedy, a battle between lust and love, and between the brutality of censorship and the unpredictable consequences of free expression. 'It's not everyone's cup of tea,' Caine admitted shortly after the film's release. 'But it's good and says some important things.' One of those important subjects was pornography, and *Quills* attempted to portray the subject in a positive light, as the film instructed, liberated and aroused all at once.

'I was attracted to the project because it had a good script, a great director, a great cast. But when I first read through my part,

I thought this man is so evil, there is nowhere to go with it. Then I read it again, and I began to find the way,' says Caine. 'I like playing characters who are sinister, but I look for a way to give them some kind of redeeming qualities. I play villains on the principle that no man is a villain to himself. All villains think they are nice people.'

Philip Kaufman, the director, believes that 'Michael Caine is so much against type in this role that he gives it a charge. We spoke of his character in terms of being a Kenneth-Starr-like man who believes he's doing a wonderful thing by ridding society of Sade's writing.' During principle photography Kaufman made the unusual decision to shoot *Quills* in chronological order to allow for further character development. 'When you create one scene after another the relationships develop organically, changing subtly from what has come before,' said Kaufman.

> **"I play villains on the principle that no man is a villain to himself. All villains think they are nice people "**

Marquis De Sade books remained officially banned in France well into the Sixties, and his books still show up on lists of banned reading material. But Kaufman kept the emphasis on fun, making a piece of Gothic-style entertainment, bringing out the comedy but allowing the

dark undertones of the story to boil
underneath. *Quills* gave Caine
another chance to stretch his
acting ability. As the end of the
century loomed large, he was
taking on more unusual roles that
showcased his talents and
provided him with new challenges.

Shiner

(2000)

Drama UK Colour 99mins

Michael Caine, Martin Landau, Frances
Barber, Frank Harper, Andy Serkis,
Claire Rushbrook, Daniel Webb,
Matthew Marsden

Director: John Irvin
Producer: Geoffrey Reeve
Screenplay: Scott Cherry

In this film of 2000, Caine plays small-time 'big ideas' boxing promoter Billy 'Shiner' Simpson, whose last shot at fame and cash goes wrong, precipitating his descent into a bloody hell. The family finances rest upon his gibbering wreck of a son defeating the relaxed American champ in the ring. No chance. Simpson's son is first knocked out and then shot, leading Simpson to root out the people who 'got his boy'. The film was reportedly based on Shakespeare's King Lear. 'I've never read King Lear,' admits Caine, 'but I'm told the story is similar because it's about a man whose family betrays him. It's not so much a gangster film but a film about a gangster.'

In the beginning, the film has a slight touch of comedy but becomes increasingly dark as the story unfolds, culminating in a blood-splattering finale. One scene in particular sees Caine's character trapped in a basement flat, holding a gun to the belly of a pregnant woman on the edge of giving birth. Caine told *Times* journalist Ginny Dougary, 'The whole thing about the movie is that it is accurate, but it's accurate about stuff you don't know about … that even newspapers can't find out about.' In fact, it was director John Irvin's

> **I'm a Londoner and most of the people on this picture are Londoners. So we've had entire conversations in rhyming slang**

intention to avoid giving the picture a glamourized look like other recent gangster flicks, such as *Lock Stock and Two Smoking Barrels*. Caine believes this worked: 'I can't imagine anyone seeing this film and then saying "I want to be a gangster"'.

Billy Shiner was a made-to-measure part for Caine: 'If I can't play this role I might as well not be an actor.' He based the part on a gangster he knew. The role was an emotional one for him not only because the character calls for rage and tragedy but also because 'There are people in *Shiner* that were like my early neighbours. And if life hadn't taken a different turn I could have been a gangster just like my character.'

Shortly after production wrapped Caine is recorded as saying: 'This has been a very special picture for me. Firstly, I was involved right from the start, collaborating with Geoff. And also this is my milieu. I'm a Londoner and most of the people on this picture are Londoners. So we've had entire conversations in rhyming slang!'

Watching Caine in his natural environment is a treat. And

although the critics were kind to Caine in their appraisal of his performance, the film itself was not much rated. Nor was it a success in the States, with Caine surmising, 'English gangster pictures don't go down that well in America … they're not convinced that English people can be gangsters.' Well, Caine knows differently.

"
If I can't play this role I might as well not be an actor
"

Miss Congeniality

(2000)

Comedy US Colour 110 mins

Sandra Bullock, Michael Caine,
Benjamin Bratt, Candice Bergen,
Ernie Hudson, William Shatner
Director: Donald Petrie
Producer: Sandra Bullock and Katie Ford
Screenplay: Marc Lawrence, Katie Ford
and Caryn Lucas

After a string of low-budget art-house pictures, which reinvented Michael Caine as an actor, Caine returned triumphantly to the Hollywood scene with *Miss Congeniality*.

Directed by Donald Petrie, *Miss Congeniality* featured Sandra Bullock in the leading role, which attracted Caine to the project. 'I've always liked Sandra's screen persona. This role is kind of zany, way-out, cuckoo kind of character that she does so well,' he said during production. 'This is the kind of film I want to see Sandra Bullock in, even if I wasn't in it…. Because she is so funny. She does little things which just make you laugh.'

After reading the script Caine agreed straight away. 'What I liked about the role was that it was funny, it was different and it was a comedy,' Caine said 'In my most recent films, I played the man who destroyed the Marquis de Sade, an abortionist and a very violent gangster.' Caine admitted: 'I was dying to get a laugh on the set.'

The plot is simple: with a bomb threat hanging over the 'Miss New Jersey' beauty pageant, an FBI agent has to go undercover to stop the crime. 'We take the most awkward, uncongenial person you've ever met in your life, and watch her transform into Miss Congeniality,' says Caine. Although the film is essentially about a beauty pageant, the filmmakers saw it as a backdrop rather than the subject.

Caine's character, Victor Melling, allowed the actor to have a lot of fun. 'Victor is on his last legs as a beauty queen adviser, which is why, when the FBI is looking for someone, he's the only one who is

available,' Caine explained during production. 'Victor will teach anybody how to be a beauty queen the same way Henry Higgins turns Eliza Doolittle into a proper lady. He's got all these little tricks that I now know, but which I didn't know before.'

When asked what she thought it would be like working with Caine, Bullock replied: 'Oh my God,

Michael Caine is going to be touching my boobs, and I was like how do you calm yourself about that? You just got to do your job. Michael Caine's got his hand down my shirt. He was like a doctor. "Ok and cut". No sweat.'

" **Michael Caine is going to be touching my boobs...how do you calm yourself about that?** "

Last Orders

(2001)

Drama UK/Colour 109 Mins

Michael Caine, Tom Courtenay,
David Hemmings, Bob Hoskins,
Helen Mirren, Ray Winstone
Director: Fred Schepisi
Producers: Nik Powell, Elisabeth
Robinson and Fred Schepisi
Screenplay: Fred Schepisi and
Graham Swift from his novel

Last Orders brought together the
very best of British acting talent,
including Bob Hoskins, Helen
Mirren, Tom Courtenay, Ray
Winstone and Michael Caine.
Directed by Fred Schepisi, the
film was based on Graham
Swift's Booker Prize-winning
novel.

Jack (Michael Caine) has died.
We join a group of his friends
who gather to scatter his ashes
and pay their last respects. The
journey to scatter the ashes takes
them not only through the English
countryside but also on a
nostalgia trip of good times and
bad times, with long-held and
long-suppressed feelings coming
to the surface. As Caine says, 'It's
about a group of blokes, the kind
you see in any pub, sitting in the
same chairs every evening. They
all know each other and seem
perfectly ordinary, but that's what's
so clever about the story, it gets
right inside these people. Nothing
is what you imagine it to be, from
the dramatic to the very funny. No
matter how ordinary people may
look, no-one is ordinary and no-
one leads an ordinary life.'

Schepisi adapted Swift's novel as
early as 1997, the actors then
committing to the project in 1998.
All of the key players involved felt
the script was an actor's dream.

'It's a little gem. I remember the
first read through, everything felt
right and everybody was so good,'
recalls Caine. As director, Schepisi
received great praise from Caine:
'He is a man for layers. When
you're doing a take, he'll cut and
remind us that we've got a back
story to remember ... He's such a

Caine's character dies in St Thomas's Hospital, the very place his own father died.

For Caine, shooting in Peckham was a case of déjà vu, as he described during filming: 'Four hundred yards down the road from where we are filming in Peckham is Wilson's Grammar School, the school I attended. I've gone full circle … from Hollywood, the bright lights and the Academy Awards, back to Peckam after forty years in the movies.'

Last Orders was a further example of Michael Caine's acting ability. He was showcasing his diverse range as an actor, from serious ensemble character pictures, to gangster films, to Hollywood chic flicks. But this role couldn't have been more different to the script that Caine was about to accept next.

I've gone full circle … from Hollywood, the bright lights and the Academy Awards, back to Peckam after forty years in the movies

delicate director and absolutely right for the story, which is personality, relationship and character driven.'

Caine thought about his character carefully: 'I based Jack on about thirty people I have known, twenty of them were related to me. These kind of characters are always full of humour – you get them in the working classes. In order to get over the misery of being poor you try to have a laugh.' Schepisi felt Caine's character was close to home: 'Ironically, he always said he would play his father one day';

Austin Powers in Goldmember

(2002)

Comedy Adventure US/ Colour

94 Mins

Mike Myers, Beyonce Knowles,
Michael Caine, Seth Green,
Michael York, Robert Wagner,
Mindy Sterling, Verne Troyer

Director: Jay Loach

Producers: John Lyons, Eric McLeod,
Demi Moore, Mike Myers,
Jennifer Todd, Suzanne Todd
and Jay Roach

Screenwriter: Mike Myers
and Michael McCullers

Goldmember was the third
instalment of the highly successful
Austin Powers franchise starring
Mike Myers as the grooviest
secret agent in movie history.

Austin Powers is once again hot
on the heels of Dr Evil, who has
teamed up with baddie
Goldmember to hatch a time-
travelling scheme to take over
the world, one that involves the
kidnapping of Nigel Powers,
Austin's beloved father and
England's most renowned spy. As
he chases the villains through
time, Austin visits 1975 and joins
forces with his old flame, Foxxy
Cleopatra, a streetwise and
stylish detective. Together Austin
and Foxxy must find a way to
rescue Nigel, and stop Dr Evil
and Goldmember from
creating mayhem.

According to the filmmakers there
was never a question as to who
should play Nigel Powers.
Michael Caine as Harry Palmer
had been one of the many
reference points Mike Myers and
director Jay Loach had turned to
when creating the original movie.
'Michael Caine was always part
of the heritage of the film. It was
perfect for Michael to be Austin's
father; it was completely organic,
a sort of poetic justice that took
us all by surprise. When he and
Mike [Myers] were on set
together, they were like twins,'
recalls Roach. As if to illustrate
that point, Roach included a
number of inspired flashbacks to
Austin and Dr Evil's past at school
in 1958, which even included
some fantastic stock footage of
Caine taken from *Alfie* to
illustrate a younger Nigel Powers.

Caine was overjoyed when he
was asked to join the cast,
having enjoyed the previous two
Austin Power's pictures, and was
more than ready for a part like
this. 'I've never done a comedy as
outrageous as this. I thought it
was a tremendous challenge,
which proved to be a helter-
skelter ride … In every actor
there is a ham waiting to get out,
and I found the ham in me,' joked
Caine during the production of the
film. Myers also enjoyed the
experience of starring opposite
one of his life-long heroes: 'He
loved putting on the glasses and
the teeth, and then loved to
complain about the teeth, which
was very funny when he tried to
say dirty words.'

Caine literally turned to the Austin
Powers character for inspiration
when bringing personality to his
own role: 'I copied as many of the
mannerisms of Austin as possible,
based on the fact that Austin
would have copied them from
Nigel.' As Caine concluded about
his character: 'I think Nigel is a
con man … he's conned
everybody…. I met a lot of real
spies when I was doing those
Harry Palmer films and they were
always rather sleazy characters.
So is Nigel.'

The scene for which Caine will be
most remembered in this movie, is

that in which Austin and Nigel banter using East-End cockney rhyming slang. As Caine remembered: 'I'm an expert on that dialogue! Myers is very knowledgeable about England, because as a comedian he's toured all the music halls so there's no colloquialism he doesn't understand.'

Austin Powers in Goldmember is considered by many to be the best Austin films to date, with the cast sharing a genuine chemistry. Caine is class in a glass, displaying none of his 69 years as he sends up the whole affair as well as the rest of the cast.

In every actor there is a ham waiting to get out, and I found the ham in me

The Quiet American

(2002)

Comedy Adventure US

Colour 94 mins

Michael Caine, Brendan Fraser,
Do Thi Hai Yen, Rade Serbedzija

Director: Philip Noyce

Producer: Staffan Ahrenberg and
William Horberg

Screenplay: Christopher Hamton and
Robert Schenkkan from the novel by
Graham Greene

Love, politics, and intrigue all intermingle in this retelling of Graham Greene's classic novel *The Quiet American*.

American aid worker Alden Pyle (Brendan Fraser) arrives in Saigon during the fall of the city in 1952, at the height of the Vietnamese fight for independence from French colonial rule. Caine is the world-weary London *Times* correspondent Thomas Fowler. He befriends the young American, but Pyle soon falls for the journalist's young Vietnamese mistress Phuong (Hai Yen). The three soon become involved in a tempestuous love triangle coated in political intrigue.

The Quiet American took several years to get off the ground, but the first break occurred when Caine agreed to come on board. 'The phone rang, and somebody said, "You were born to play Thomas Fowler",' recalls Caine. 'I've been married to the same woman for 30 years, and this guy is supposed to be off in the Far East with a 22 year old and he's supposed to be 58. So I thought "Well…it's probably a complement!" '

As director Philip Noyce says, 'Casting Caine was crucial…. He brings enormous empathy to the character of Fowler. Michael has the capacity to open up his heart to an audience and it's very important that we have a Fowler who people can empathize with.' Caine says that he found the inspiration for his character in Greene himself: 'I met Greene a couple of times and I'm kind of basing myself on him'. He also

> **The phone rang, and somebody said, "You were born to play Thomas Fowler"**

spent time with a journalist on location, who had been a London *Times* correspondent during the Vietnamese conflict.

Before completing location work in Hanoi and returning to the Fox Studios in Sydney, the cast and crew spent four days in the remote town of Ninh Binh, which, as Caine recalls, was an experience in itself: 'It was the most difficult location to work in. It was freezing cold and pouring with rain and we were slushing around in mud for days. We looked like soldiers. I used to be a solider so I know what it's like … it didn't bother me.' However, he found his experience in Vietnam incredibly rewarding: 'Vietnam is more beautiful than you imagine because your imaginings have been clouded over. You say "Vietnam" and you think of war and death, but of course the war has been gone for a long time. It is a very, very beautiful place and the people are rewarding.'

The Quiet American struggled for recognition from its US distributor, Miramax Films, who were concerned at the perceived anti-American tone of the movie, and it was Caine who stepped in and persuaded studio boss Harvey Weinstein that the film deserved a shot. 'The film was shown to Miramax on Sept 10th 2001, in New York. The next day I was waiting for Philip Noyce to ring and tell me how it had gone when the planes went into the Twin Towers and I realized that I wouldn't be hearing from anybody for a couple of months.' Caine was soon told the film wouldn't get a theatrical release until January 2003. 'That is like saying we have put it in the garbage can.' Michael persuaded Weinstein to open the film in Toronto and see what the reception was like; after all, the picture wasn't as political as some thought. 'I said that if the people in Toronto say it is crap, I will come back in January and bring a shovel and help you bury it, but I also asked that if they say it is good, will you get behind it? He said yes, and he has been as good as his word.'

Oscar nominated for the fourth time in his career for Best Actor, the prize was not his in the end, this time it went to Adrien Brody for his performance in Polanski's *The Pianist*.

The Actors

(2003)

Comedy UK Colour 91 mins

Michael Caine, Dylan Moran,
Michael Gambon, Lena Headey,
Miranda Richardson

Director: Conor McPherson

Producers: Stephen Woolley, Neil
Jordan, Redmond Morris

Screenplay: Conor McPherson, from
an original story by Neil Jordan

After *The Quiet American*, Michael Caine turned his attention back to comedy, this time in the form of Irish-inspired *The Actors*, which was greeted with mixed reviews.

Directed by Dublin-born Conor McPherson, the movie tells the story of two rather eccentric actors Tom (Dylan Moran) and O'Malley (Michael Caine) who prove the little-known adage that bad actors make good crooks. For his research into the character of Richard III, O'Malley hangs out with local criminals in the roughest pub in town and is embroiled in a farcical plot to steal a large sum, with the help of Tom and Tom's clever 9-year-old niece, Mary.

With Dylan Moran signed, director Conor McPherson suggested to the producers that they ask Michael Caine to taken on the older character, O'Malley. Two of the producers had previously worked with Caine, Woolley producing *Mona Lisa* and Jordan directing the same film. 'I couldn't believe it when we sent him the script and he said he wanted to do it,' says McPherson. 'Like all good actors he's very competitive … he takes no shit from anyone and I think we recognized a certain stubbornness in one another, which ironically really helped us to get along and work well.' However, McPherson was nervous of working with Caine: 'I would be lying if I said I wasn't intimidated. I mean when a man is telling you stories from films like Woody Allen's *Hannah And Her Sisters* and John Huston's *The Man Who Would Be King*, it's sort of mind blowing.'

After a run of serious work Caine was keen to sink his teeth into another comedy. 'You always look very carefully at a script when it's comedy – for every ten dramatic scripts you only get one good comedy. Conor is such a clever writer, he writes terrific dialogue. The script made me laugh out loud and that hasn't happened to me since *Dirty Rotten Scoundrels*,' said Caine.

Caine had great fun with the part. 'I got to play a duff Richard III with a hunchback and a big nose.

I'm sure this is the only time I will get to play Richard III, no matter how badly. I certainly won't be asked again when people see this … and I play a woman gang boss, but I look terrible as a woman. I certainly wouldn't go out with me if I looked like that.' Caine visibly enjoys the chance to slaughter Shakespeare on stage, and his comic timing is perfect.

The Actors failed to tickle the critics. They thought it was a mishmash of bad accents, with poorly thought out 'comedy' moments and a contrived story. Nobody will remember *The Actors,* but it makes no claims to fame, only to raise a few laughs.

> **The script made me laugh out loud and that hasn't happened to me since *Dirty Rotten Scoundrels***

And the rest…

The Wrong Box (1966)

Period Comedy UK Colour 101 mins
John Mills, Ralph Richardson, Michael Caine, Peter Cook, Dudley Moore,
Nanette Newman, Tony Hancock, Peter Sellers, Wilfred Lawson
Director/Producer: Bryan Forbes
Screenplay: Larry Gelbart, Burt Shevelove from the Robert Louis Stevenson novel

Directed by Bryan Forbes, *The Wrong Box* was based on
the Robert Louis Stevenson novel and featured some of
the best British comedy performers of the Sixties. The daft
plot involved John Mills trying to kill Ralph Richardson
over an inheritance, and amongst the likes of Peter Sellers,
Tony Hancock and Dudley Moore, Caine held his own.

Director Forbes told film writer Michael Freedland:
'Michael proved…an extraordinary actor – a chameleon
in many ways. He came to *The Wrong Box* after *Alfie*,
Zulu and *The Ipcress File*. He always showed up, no side,
no temperament, no bullshit.'

Woman Times Seven (1967)

Comedy Drama US Colour 103mins
Shirley Maclaine, Alan Arkin, Peter Sellers, Rossano Brazzi, Vittorio
Gassman, Michael Caine
Director: Vittorio De Sica
Producer: Arthur Cohn
Screenplay: Cesare Zavattini

Woman Times Seven was Caine's first cameo
performance. Shot in Paris, the movie starred Shirley
MacLaine in seven vignettes, paired with or pitted
against seven different men. Caine appeared as a private
detective for the best part of three minutes on screen
time and no dialogue.

'I did this as a favour to Shirley, in return for the one she
had done me by taking me to Hollywood for the first
time,' says Caine. But he also had other reasons. He
wanted to work with director Vittorio De Sica. 'He acted
out my part for me before we started shooting and I was
amazed. I'm not sure my performance on camera was
anywhere as good as his off camera'.

Michael relished location, his first shot was on the
Champs Elysees 'I could actually sit and have breakfast
in Fouquet's, one of my favourite restaurants, and watch
the crew set up the shot.'

Deadfall (1968)

Crime thriller UK Colour 126 mins
Michael Caine, Giovanna Ralli, Eric Portman,
Nanette Newman, David Buck, Carlos Pierre
Director: Bryan Forbes
Producer: Paul Monash
Screenplay: Bryan Forbes from the novel by Desmond Cory

Deadfall was the second time Michael Caine worked
with director Bryan Forbes, and the result proved even
worse than their previous collaboration, *The Wrong Box*.

Caine played a cat burglar who teams up with a married couple to rob a multi-millionaire. His character soon falls in love with the wife, whose husband turns out to be gay. The film made the mistake of focusing too much on the love entanglements rather than the caper.

As *Deadfall* was to be shot in Majorca, Caine approached the project enthusiastically: 'I was all set for a wonderful experience, but it didn't work out that way. Somehow between the writing of the script and the shooting of the film, something important got lost.'

However dire the reviews for *Deadfall*, the film was blessed with a wonderful score from composer John Barry, whose luscious guitar music during the robbery proved to be one of the film's only saving graces.

The Magus (1968)

Fantasy Drama UK Colour 116 mins
Anthony Quinn, Michael Caine, Candice Bergen, Anna Karina, Paul Stassino, Julian Glover, Takis Emmanuel, George Pastell, Daniele Noel
Director: Guy Green
Producer: John Kohn and Jud Kinberg
Screenplay: John Fowles, from his book

Asked whether he would do anything the same if he were to live his life again, Peter Sellers commented: 'Yes. But I wouldn't see *The Magus*.'

John Fowles' novel is like marmite: you either love it or hate it. Although a cult book, particularly in the late Sixties and early Seventies (Jodie Foster claims it is her favourite book of all time), Caine admits that he has difficulty understanding any of Fowles' work, and even after the script had reportedly been simplified, he still didn't have a clue what the story was about. In fact, the story centres on Englishman Nicholas Urfe, played by Caine, who arrives on a Greek island to teach English.

Shot on the Spanish island of Majorca, *The Magus* was the first of a two-picture deal Caine had with Twentieth Century Fox, both of which he considers, on reflection, as disasters. 'I did not want to make the picture but I had to under the phantom contract,' he declared in his autobiography. He tried to show more enthusiasm when the cameras began rolling. 'They said it would all come right in the cutting room … but it didn't'.

Caine was starring opposite actor Anthony Quinn, whose entourage would arrive on the set before the actor and inform his co-stars what mood Quinn happened to be in. One morning Caine retorted, 'Has he ever asked what mood I'm in?' From that moment the pair got on well, and working with Quinn is Caine's only fond memory of the occasion. They would later co-star in *The Marseille Contract*.

Play Dirty (1969)

World War II drama UK Colour 113 mins
Michael Caine, Nigel Davenport, Nigel Green, Harry Andrews, Bernard Archard, Daniel Pilon
Director: Andre De Toth
Screenplay: Lotte Colin and Melvyn Bragg, from a story by George Marton

Play Dirty was the first of several war movies Caine made during the late Sixties and early Seventies. Caine had a clear motive for taking the role of Captain Douglas, an inexperienced officer leading a unit to blow up an enemy fuel dump in North Africa during World War II: 'I would never appear in a war film that made any young man feel like going out and joining the army … that was part of the reason I played in *Play Dirty*.'

Filming was originally planned for Israel, but once the producers discovered this would become an insurance nightmare, the movie was relocated to Spain, which had become a popular location for many spaghetti westerns. In fact, with only four big sand dunes in Almeria the location had its limitations. On one particular day director Andre De Toth was capturing shots of Rommel's Afrika Korps advancing across the desert towards El Alamein, only to be greeted over the hill by a stagecoach chased by American Indians.

The script was co-written by Melvyn Bragg years before his television career had started and he received more critical acclaim for his novels. Bragg may well want to forget this project. As Caine admits: '*Play Dirty* is a good example of how you can start off with a good story and the very best of intentions and yet get gradually worn down into mediocrity.'

Too Late The Hero (1970)

World War II drama US Colour 133 mins
Michael Caine, Cliff Robertson, Ian Bannen, Harry Andrews, Henry Fonda, Denholm Elliot, Ronald Fraser
Director/Producer: Robert Aldrich
Screenplay: Robert Aldrich and Lukas Heller, from a story by Robert Aldrich and Robert Sherman

Too Late The Hero, director Robert Aldrich's attempt to re-create his *Dirty Dozen* success, turned out to be a tough and gruelling filmmaking experience for Caine. Focusing on the World War II battle for a small, unnamed Pacific island, a group of commandos are dispatched on a suicide mission to destroy the enemy wireless station hidden deep in the jungle.

Aldrich was happy with Caine in the lead role: 'He was superb in that picture … the trouble was he was

working with an asshole co-star.' The studio advised Aldrich to shoot two endings, one, for the US market, which featured Cliff Robertson surviving the battle, the other with Michael Caine as last man standing for UK audiences. He didn't. In the final cut Robertson was given a dramatic death, leaving Caine as the only survivor.

Living only on a diet of tinned sardines and cheese, the unit spent six months in the Philippines. The location was hell. 'Bob had us work for 14 consecutive days and then gave us five days off, which was enough time to get out of the country,' remembers Caine. On reflection, Caine says the same effect could have been achieved had Aldrich shot the picture in the tropical house at Kew Gardens: 'It was just all of us looking out from behind a load of palm leaves.'

Zee and Co (1971)

Drama UK Colour 110 mins
Elizabeth Taylor, Michael Caine, Susannah York, Margaret Leighton, John Standing, Mark Larkin
Director: Brian G Hutton
Producer: Jay Kanter and Alan Ladd Jnr
Screenplay: Edna O'Brien

When Michael Caine was offered *Zee and Co*, he almost agreed without even reading the script when he heard he was to appear opposite Elizabeth Taylor, at the time the biggest female star in the world. And Caine found his encounter with Elizabeth Taylor as entertaining as he had hoped. When she turned up on set at Shepperton Studios with a jug of Bloody Mary, he knew it would be fine. 'Elizabeth and I became great friends instantly, because she is a no-bullshit lady, and I'd like to imagine myself as a no bullshit man.'

Zee and Co, or *X, Y and Zee* as it was known in the States, was a peculiar drama about adultery, in which Caine played a successful architect whose wife leaves him for another woman. 'We made what we thought was a comedy, and everybody thought it was a drama', Caine commented. 'I thought it was a good movie, but then I don't have to pay to see it.'

The critics loathed it. 'It was very much a woman's picture and a little ahead of its time,' says Caine musing over the film's failure. 'It was, to say the least, not quite my style of thing, but I really wanted to work with Elizabeth so I took it and never regretted it.'

The Wilby Conspiracy (1975)

Political thriller UK Colour 101 mins
Sidney Poitier, Michael Caine, Nicol Williamson,
Prunella Gee, Persis Khambatta
Director: Ralph Nelson
Producer: Martin Baum
Screenplay: Rod Amateau and Harold Nebenzal, from
the novel by Peter Driscoll

The Wilby Conspiracy was Michael Caine's first foray into what he called 'message pictures', telling biographer William Hall, 'I did that part purely because of the anti-Apartheid angle.' He had experienced first-hand the Apartheid system when he shot *Zulu* in South Africa, and since then had been disgusted by the regime. Sidney Poitier plays a political activist, who embarks on a cross-country flight from the law, dragging an unwilling Michael Caine with him.

Not surprisingly, shooting the film in South Africa was a no-no for safety reasons, so principle photography took place in Kenya. Caine was, however, nearly killed during a scene in which he was sitting in the passenger seat of

a car being driven by Poitier at speed. A bolt loosened on the camera fixed to the bonnet. 'Luckily there was no windscreen, and no flying glass, just a camera exploding between us'.

The Wilby Conspiracy was a genuine effort at trying to convey Apartheid rule. However, neither critics nor audiences gave the film the thumbs up. Poitier and Caine would eventually team up again in the late Nineties, for another saga on the subject, *Mandela and De Klerk*.

Peeper (1975)

Detective comedy US Colour 83 mins
Michael Caine, Natalie Wood, Kitty Winn, Thayer David,
Liam Dunn, Dorothy Adams
Director: Peter Hyams
Producer: Irwin Winkler and Robert Chartoff
Screenplay: WD Richter, from the novel *Deadfall* by Keith Laumer

Four Michael Caine films were released in 1975, and not all of them can be considered classics: *Peeper* certainly wasn't vintage stuff. Caine said shortly after the film's failure: 'I have the cardinal fault of not only making mistakes – I have to repeat them. *Peeper* just didn't work.'

Caine played LA-based private investigator Leslie Tucker, who is hired to find somebody's long lost daughter and to present her with a suitcase of money. Tucker discovers that a wealthy woman adopted the child, but finds two grown-up daughters each claiming to be the heir. The picture starred Natalie Wood, who spends most of her screen time parading around a palace in a skimpy white silk dress.

Peeper was another production Caine said he enjoyed for the location: after all, part of the shoot required a trip to the Caribbean on a cruise liner. Shot under the title *Fat Chance*, the film's release was a low-key affair, reportedly lying dormant at Twentieth Century Fox for a year before a heavily edited version was released.

Harry and Walter Go To New York (1976)

Crime Caper US Colour 106 mins
James Caan, Elliott Gould, Michael Caine, Diane Keaton, Charles Durning, Lesley Ann Warren, Val Avery, Jack Gilford
Director: Mark Rydell
Producer: Tony Bill
Screenplay: John Byrum and Robert Kaufman

Blessed with a glittering cast, this period bank heist simply didn't live up to expectations. Joined by entertainers-turned-safecrackers James Caan and Elliott Gould, Michael Caine plays the mastermind of the operation, with Diane Keaton thrown in as the love interest. At that time in their careers, all three actors were working at a frantic pace, each making at least three films a year. It shows.

As Caine remembers, 'The whole cast was bananas, and so was the director. It was one of those films which was so fun to do, and with such clever people, that it should have been a great movie.' It doesn't always work out that way. Some critics went so far as to call the film embarrassing: a comedy that wasn't funny. Director Mark Rydell said he started out with the intention of making a Laurel and Hardy picture with real people. The film was quickly forgotten. In fact, Caine doesn't even mention it in his autobiography.

The Eagle Has Landed (1976)

World War II adventure US Colour 117 mins
Michael Caine, Donald Sutherland, Robert Duvall, Jenny Agutter, Donald Pleasence, Anthony Quayle, Jean Marsh, John Standing, Judy Geeson
Director: John Sturges
Producer: Jack Wiener and David Niven Jr
Screenplay: Tom Mankiewicz, from the novel by Jack Higgins

Directed by veteran John Sturges, who was responsible for some of the all-time classics, including *The Great Escape* and *The Magnificent Seven*, *The Eagle Has Landed* was adapted by James Bond screenwriter Tom Mankiewicz from Jack Higgins' novel.

Michael Caine plays a German colonel leading a task force who infiltrate an English village in 1943, with the aim of kidnapping Winston Churchill. He explained his character to biographer William Hall: 'I play the heavy in the picture, and it's not one of the easiest to play – a sympathetic soldier. He was a German paratroop officer from old family German aristocracy who hated the Gestapo and the Nazis who were considered nouveau riche and bourgeois opportunists, working-class yobbos.'

Caine and the rest of the cast were very pleased to be working for such a renowned director, until that is, they discovered that Sturges couldn't wait to leave the project. The director was only interested in continuing his deep-sea fishing, and, now in his later years, would never follow a picture through its editing and post-production processes. 'I still get angry when I think of what it could have been with the right director,' reflects Caine.

The Silver Bears (1977)

Comedy Adventure US Colour 107 mins
Michael Caine, Cybill Shepherd, Louis Jordon,
Stephanie Audran, David Warner, Martin Balsam, Jay Leno, Tony Mascia,
Joss Ackland, Tom Smothers, Charles Gray, Jeremy Clyde
Director: Ivan Passer
Producer: Arlene Sellers and Alex Winitsky
Screenplay: Peter Stone, from the novel by Paul E Erdman

Michael Caine plays Doc Fletcher, who sets up a bank scam in Switzerland, for gangster Martin Balsam, and soon becomes involved in a swindle, involving an Iranian silver mine. Caine liked the role, 'It was very light and charming'.

Aware of the film's subject matter, *The Evening Standard* reported that while making *The Silver Bears*, Caine had the latest share prices and exchange rates telephoned to him each night. He told the London newspaper, 'I take an interest in everything political and economic, because I know it's going to effect to me, and I like to stay ahead of the game.'

Caine had just purchased a new property, a house that needed a lot of work (and money), so he admits he took *The Silver Bears* because it was the first project that came his way. One critic remarked: 'If your idea of a good laugh is watching Caine spill his breakfast onto his lap – twice in a row – this is your movie.'

The Jigsaw Man (1984)

Spy drama UK Colour 90mins
Michael Caine, Laurence Olivier, Susan George,
Robert Powell, Charles Gray, Michael Medwin
Director: Terence Young
Producer: Bob Porter
Screenplay: Jo Eisinger, from the novel by Dorothea Bennet

Although Laurence Olivier and Caine were together again, this Cold War thriller didn't have the impact of *Sleuth*, 12 years earlier. The story centres on British traitor Sir Philip Kimberly, played by Caine, whose face is surgically altered by the Russians so that he can be sent back to the West on a mission.

The surreal opening scene has Caine's voice emerging from the mouth of an unknown face. Wheeled into an operating theatre, the stranger has the bandages removed and the familiar face materializes from Russian plastic surgery. But the rest of Young's film doesn't live up to this exciting opening.

The Jigsaw Man was put together on a tight budget; it was so stretched there were reports that there wasn't enough money to pay the cast. Olivier took his attorney's advice and walked off the set, and the remaining six days of principle photography were postponed for six months. In true form, Caine managed to squeeze in two more films in the meantime.

Veteran director Terence Young, responsible for three James Bond films, was left to try and put this impossible 'jigsaw' film together. The picture went straight to video. Caine made the movie for one simple reason: 'I did it to work with Larry again.'

Water (1985)

Comedy UK Colour 93 mins
Michael Caine, Valerie Perrine, Brenda Vaccaro,
Leonard Rossiter, Billy Connolly, Dennis Duggan, Fulton Mackay,
Jimmie Walker, Dick Shawn, Fred Gwynne
Director: Dick Clement
Producer: Ian La Frenais
Screenplay: Dick Clement, Ian La Frenais and Bill Persky,
from *Persky's Story*

Handmade Films made some of the most talked about

British pictures of the Eighties, but it was movies like *Water* that contributed to the company's eventual demise.

Caine portrays a British diplomat on a Caribbean island, a small dependency forgotten by Whitehall, that is, until a resident, played by Billy Connolly, attempts to enlist the help of Cuba in his struggle for independence. Matters become complicated by the last-minute discovery that the island has a valuable source of mineral water.

Although written by British sitcom writers Dick Clement and Ian La Frenais, who also took on the roles of director and producer respectively, the film was unsuccessful. Some critics went so far as to say the film was unwatchable. Caught up in this ludicrous tale, Michael Caine once again manages to emerge with reputation intact, although it is a strong contender for the worst Caine movie of all time.

The Holcroft Covenant (1985)

Spy thriller UK Colour 107 mins
Michael Caine, Anthony Andrews, Victoria Tennant,
Lilli Palmer, Mario Adorf, Michael Lonsdale
Director: John Frankenheimer
Producers: Mort Abrahams, Edie Landau and Ely A. Landau
Screenplay: George Axel Rod, Edward Anhalt and John Hopkins, from the novel by Robert Ludlam

The Holcroft Covenant was a classic 'Caine stinker'. 'It sounded like a winner … Wrong again,' Caine admitted in his autobiography. And he was harsh on the outcome: 'It went straight down the toilet.' He accepted the role on the last day of shooting *Water*, after James Caan backed out at the last minute. In fact, it all happened so quickly there was no time even for wardrobe fittings and Caine ended up wearing his own clothes in the picture. He didn't even have time to read the script. Once principle

photography began, he realized, 'I couldn't understand the plot, so God help the poor audience who would eventually see it.'

Based on Robert Ludlum's novel, *The Holcroft Covenant* saw Caine playing architect Noel Holcroft, a foreign-born American citizen who discovers that he has inherited half a billion dollars of ex-Nazi money from his father, a Nazi officer, who committed suicide at the end of the war. Frankenheimer, the director, rated Caine's acting ability highly but didn't utilize the actor to the full.

Michael Caine's atrocious stint of films was beginning to show. One journalist pointed out that he had made more bad films than anyone else. Caine replied: 'That's because I've made more films than anyone else.'

Sweet Liberty (1986)

Comedy US Colour 101 mins
Alan Alda, Michael Caine, Michelle Pfeiffer,
Bob Hoskins, Lise Hilboldt, Lillian Gish
Director: Alan Alda
Producer: Martin Bergman
Screenplay: Alan Alda

Sweet Liberty is an enjoyable, undemanding piece of entertainment, telling the story of a film within a film. Alan Alda wrote, directed and starred in the movie, playing an academic whose historical novel on the American War of Independence is being made into a film. Alda claimed he wrote the part of the big-headed actor especially for Caine, who joked in his memoirs: 'My role was of a conceited, arrogant movie star – a part I found strangely accessible and for which I had done masses of research.' Alda found that working with Caine was '… like being with a combination of Laurence Olivier and Art Buchwald.'

Joining Caine was old friend Bob Hoskins, ex-Bond girl Lois Chiles and newcomer Michelle Pfeiffer. Recalls Caine: 'Michelle was not yet the enormous star she is today and I remember being surprised that someone who was such a stunning beauty and could act so well, had not already made it.'

Caine's role was a gift, and the critics loved him as the womanizer, stealing the show with a scene in which he leads his co-stars in a rousing rendition of 'Knees Up, Mother Brown!'. He clearly relished the part.

Half Moon Street (1986)

Political thriller UK Colour 85 mins
Sigourney Weaver, Michael Caine, Patrick Kavanagh, Faith Kent, Ram John Holder, Keith Buckley
Director: Bob Swaim
Producer: Geoffrey Reeve
Screenplay: Edward Behr and Bob Swaim, from the novel *Doctor Slaughter* by Paul Theroux

Half Moon Street was director Bob Swaim's first English-language picture. Coming from the French film industry, Swaim explained the difficulty that budget limitation placed on the film. 'It's $6,000,000 to make the movie, which includes a lot of other things. There's X amount of dollars below the line. In France, for example, 75% of the budget is on the screen. Of course, when you're working with Michael Caine and Sigourney Weaver, you're already into major stars and a lot of that money is not on the screen.'

Weaver plays a doctor who arrives in London ready to take up a position at one of the city's institutes after completing a three-year field study in China. The paycheck isn't wonderful and she soon finds herself as a high-class escort. One of her clients is a lonely widower played by Michael Caine.

Rather than promoting Michael Caine, the studio tried to ride on the name of Sigourney Weaver, who was fresh from the success of *Alien*. All the same, the film failed miserably at the box office. Caine has never had much to say about the picture, but he did send his co-star, Weaver, to collect his Oscar for *Hannah And Her Sisters* while he was busy shooting *Jaws: The Revenge* in the Bahamas.

The Whistle Blower (1986)

Spy thriller UK Colour 99 mins
Michael Caine, James Fox, Nigel Havers, John Gielgud, Felicity Dean
Director: Simon Langton
Producer: Geoffrey Reeve
Screenplay: Julian Bond, from the novel by John Hale

Michael Caine accepted the role in *The Whistle Blower* for less than his usual fee, part of his policy to encourage new talent, which this time was director Simon Langston. It was the second of two 'gritty thrillers' he made in the UK in 1986, the other being *The Fourth Protocol.*

Caine plays Frank Jones in this low-key but satisfying thriller. He is investigating the mysterious death of his son, played by Nigel Havers, who had worked as a Russian translator at the GCHQ. Caine's performance as a veteran of the Korean War is convincing, as he enters a creepy world of whispers and a seemingly impenetrable wall of class privilege and secrecy. During production Caine said, 'It's the little man up against the Establishment. Not a hero, just a normal human being.' He felt the movie's subject matter was particularly interesting: 'I was told of a number of suicides among scientists working on secret projects, so perhaps there's something going on.'

The Whistle Blower showcased Caine's acting ability, with the detail that makes his performances so special. When informed of his son's death, there isn't even a flicker in Caine's eye, this subtle approach conveying the devastation perfectly.

Surrender (1987)

Romantic comedy US Colour 91 mins
Sally Field, Michael Caine, Steve Guttenburg, Peter Boyle, Julie Kavner, Jackie Cooper
Director: Jerry Belson
Producer: Alan Greisman and Aaron Spelling
Screenplay: Jerry Belson

On completing filming, Michael Caine told one reporter that *Surrender* was the best film he had ever made. It bombed. 'It's always a disaster when I like a film … I thought it was funny,' he said, looking back on the movie that reunited him with *Poseidon* co-star and friend Sally Field.

In this comical romp Caine played Sean Stein, a successful novelist who's unsuccessful dealings with woman has led him to decide to have nothing to do with the opposite sex. All this changes when he falls in love with a production-line artist after attending a party, in which a gang of robbers gatecrash and order all the guests to remove their clothes.

The opening of *Surrender*, at which audiences apparently booed in some theatres, set a new Hollywood record: it was the fourth Michael Caine film to open in the space of four months. 'I used to do four films in five minutes … I was a late developer,' he joked.

Jack the Ripper (1988)

Drama based on a true story UK Colour 183 mins
Michael Caine, Armand Assante, Jane Seymour, Lewis Collins, Ray McAnally, Susan George, Harry Andrews, Lysette Anthony
Director: David Wickes
Producer: David Wickes
Screenplay: Derek Marlowe and David Wickes

Jack the Ripper was the reason Michael Caine ventured back onto the small screen for the first time in 19 years, and he enjoyed every moment of it: 'The great thing is they concentrate on you as an actor. It's your performance they are shooting, and you don't have to wait for the cavalry to come over the hill for an hour before they shoot your close-up!' However, the filming schedule took a bit of getting used to: 'It was a little brisk for someone used to the working at the leisurely pace of feature films.'

Thames Television in the UK and Lorimar in the States, who financed this two-part television movie, demanded an international star in the lead role and so Caine was hired to appear as Inspector Abberline, the real-life Scotland Yard detective who investigated the gruesome murders of East End prostitutes in the late 1880s. The drama was commissioned to coincide with the 100th anniversary of the Ripper murders and was a hit both sides of the Atlantic, achieving one of the highest rating figures in Britain that year.

Although in real life the murderer was never caught, Caine was required to shoot four different endings so there was no chance the identity of the villain could be leaked to the press; not even the actors knew until transmission. Caine was paid one million pounds and when he asked director David Wickes if he should grow a moustache for the role, the answer was simple: 'No! We've paid for the face, let's see it!'

The Strange Case of Dr Jekyll and Mr Hyde (1989)

Horror UK/US Colour 94 mins
Michael Caine, Cheryl Ladd, Joss Ackland, Ronald Pickup, Kim Thomson,
Lionel Jeffries
Director: David Wickes
Producer: Patricia Carr
Screenplay: David Wickes, from the novel *The Strange Case of Dr Jekyll and Mr Hyde* by Robert Louis Stevenson

This much-loved classic gets the American television makeover, with Michael Caine playing the split personality of the Victorian gentleman Dr Henry Jekyll and his evil counterpart Mr Edward Hyde. This bland film was the second collaboration between Caine and director David Wickes, following on from *Jack The Ripper*.

Caine says he learnt a lesson during the five-week shoot: 'The make-up for Mr Hyde took four hours to put on, and four hours to take off. It was hellishly uncomfortable. Plus, of course, nobody wanted to have lunch with me looking like that.' Caine promised that he would never make another movie that demanded this level of make-up. Caine's appearance became a source of humour for the rest of the cast, as co-star Joss Ackland confessed to film writer, Freedland: 'What I remember about that picture was that Michael walked around dressed up as a potato.'

Despite the uncomfortable make-up Caine enjoyed aspects of the shoot, especially the scenes in which he had to go berserk, smashing up labs and throwing people through windows. Some thought Caine was more than right for the part: 'I've been told I've got a Victorian face. Mind you I dislike the stiff collars, the fog and the gloom.'

A Shock To The System (1990)

Black comedy US Colour 84 mins
Michael Caine, Elizabeth McGovern, Peter Riegert, Swoosie Kurtz, Will Patton, Jenny Wright, John McMartin, Barbara Baxley, Samuel L Jackson
Director: Jan Egleson
Producer: Patrick McCormick
Screenplay: Andrew Klavan, from the novel by Simon Brett

'I'd been reading a lot of scripts, one after the other, and suddenly I read this one. I said, "Wait a minute". It's a very funny nightmare, quite frightening, but extremely funny,' said Caine after flicking through the script of *A Shock To The System*, which was directed by first timer Jan Egleson.

Caine played Graham Marshall, a talented and dedicated advertising executive, who endures mounting bills and a nagging wife. But he has one thing to look forward to: a well-deserved promotion. But when the position is given to a loud-mouthed yuppie, Marshall becomes frustrated, driving him to murder his wife. 'He's victimized and he knows it,' said Caine. 'He is pushed and pushed until he can take no more … I meet men like him all the time.'

Shot in New York, Caine recalls that the Mayor had set up a special police squad to deal specifically with film units. 'These officers have become very knowledgeable about the art of filmmaking over the years.' One night, when Caine was standing with one of the special squad, Egleson shouted: 'Cut!' 'There was a hiss of disapproval from my police friend,' Caine remembers. '"What's the matter?" I asked. "Woody would have gone in for a two-shot there," he said – and he was probably right.'

Mr Destiny (1990)

Comedy drama US Colour 105 mins
James Belushi, Linda Hamilton, Michael Caine, Jon Lovitz, Hart Bochner, Bill McCutcheon, Rene Russo
Director: James Orr
Producer: Jim Cruickshank and James Orr
Screenplay: James Orr and Jim Cruickshank

Mr Destiny steals its idea from a range of different sources (including *It's a Wonderful Life*) and it shows. For Larry Burrows (James Belushi) nothing in life has gone the way he has wanted. He's unhappy about everything from his house, to his car, to his wife. One night his car breaks down in a deserted town and he wanders into a bar. Behind the counter stands Mr Destiny (Michael Caine) who allows him to relive his life as though he had all the objects he has ever desired. As the film asks, would he have been any happier?

Caine is, once again, flawless, although we see little of him, in this low-key, slow-moving affair, which is nothing more than a fable.

Blue Ice (1992)

Thriller US/UK Colour 68 mins
Michael Caine, Sean Young, Ian Holm, Bobby Short, Alun Armstrong, Sally Kelly, Jack Shepherd, Philip Davis
Director: Russell Mulcahy
Producer: Martin Bregman and Michael Caine
Screenplay: Ron Hutchinson, from a character by Ted Allbeury

The premise of *Blue Ice* was quite simple: 'Michael Caine with a gun in his hand and a woman in the other. That's it,' as Caine puts it. 'It's a very English film,' he stressed during the making of the film, 'with all the mystery and intrigue foreigners associate with London.' The film was produced by Caine and Martin Bregman for HBO for only

$6 million. Caine said during production: 'We don't have $30 million to spend on stuntmen and explosives like they do on the *Lethal Weapons* and *Die Hards*. So what we have to spend our time on is imagination.'

Caine plays former secret agent Harry Anders, who now runs a successful jazz club in London. When he becomes involved in a minor car accident with the beautiful Stacy Mansdorf (Sean Young), wife of the American ambassador, he finds himself reluctantly pulled back into the world of espionage. It was Caine's choice to cast Sean Young of *Blade Runner* fame as his leading lady: 'Sean Young's name came up, and everybody cringed with horror … [But} She wasn't an ounce of trouble, she charmed everybody on set, down to the last technician.'

The producers were hoping that *Blue Ice* would be the first of series of movies focusing on the Harry Anders character, but audiences decided otherwise.

On Deadly Ground (1994)

Action Adventure US Colour 96 mins
Steven Seagal, Michael Caine, Joan Chen, John C McGinley, R Lee Ermey.
Director: Steven Seagal
Producer: Steven Seagal
Screenplay: Patrick Alexander

On Deadly Ground is another movie Michael Caine might choose to forget, although his camped-up part of an oil executive who is destroying Alaska's environment is quite enjoyable. His cartoon cut-out villain dressed the part with heavily dyed black eyebrows and slicked back hair. Action hero perennial Steven Seagal is called in to him stop him.

But Caine didn't enjoy making the movie one bit, clashing with director and fellow actor Steven Seagal. Caine's publicist told Michael Freedland 'He is the only man he would never want to work with again.' It has been suggested that the only reason Caine took the part was to try to tap into the younger audience following that Seagal had secured.

On Deadly Ground was Seagal's first time in the director's chair. Many critics complained at the picture's heavy-handed eco-message, as the film was stuffed with impassioned green speeches.

Mandela and de Klerk (1997)

Political drama US Colour 109 mins
Sidney Poitier, Michael Caine, Tina Lifford, Gerry Maritz, Terry Norton
Director: Joseph Sargent
Producer: Bernard Sofronski
Screenplay: Richard Wesley

In 1996, before Rafelson's *Blood and Wine* restored him to critical favour, Caine made *Mandela and de Klerk*, a television movie that told the story of how Nelson Mandela and FW de Klerk jointly earned the Nobel Peace Prize for their efforts in bringing about democracy in South Africa. To enhance the authenticity of the film, director Joseph Sargent shot the movie in locales where the Mandela/de Klerk negotiations actually took place, cut in authentic newsreel footage and hired black South African actors to play minor roles.

Caine's performance as de Klerk tries to show the unselfish pragmatism that encouraged the politician to surrender to destiny and, with Mandela, turn South Africa into a democracy.

This low-profile production earned high praise from critics for its outstanding and faithful re-creation of an important turning point in South African history. The film starred Sidney Poitier as Nelson Mandela, but it was Caine as the Afrikaner president who grabbed the attention of the critics, winning him an Emmy award in the category of Outstanding Supporting Actor in a Mini series or special. He also received a Golden Globe nomination.

Shadow Run (1998)

Crime Drama UK Colour
Michael Caine, Kenneth Colley, James Fox, Leslie Grantham, Christopher Cazenove
Director: Geoffrey Reeve
Producer: Jim Reeve
Screenplay: Desmond Lowden

Shadow Run saw Michael Caine playing the comfortable role of a British gangster once again, this time in Nineties London and exotic Hertfordshire. Caine plays the ruthless villain Haskell who teams up with an upper-class city crime lord to organize a daring attack on a high-security van with cargo worth over £110 million.

Caine teamed up once more with Geoffrey Reeve with whom he had previously collaborated on *Half Moon Street* and *The Whistle Blower*. The entire supporting cast was top drawer, and Caine produces a sterling performance. One of his famous on-screen tricks – not to blink on camera – is performed here with a chilling menace.

The movie disappeared without trace, and was directly released on video both in the UK and US. By now, many were wondering what on earth had happened to Michael Caine the movie star. But he was about to make a come back big time: in Mark Herman's *Little Voice*.

Curtain Call (1999)

Supernatural comedy US Colour 95 mins
James Spader, Michael Caine, Sam Shepard, Buck Henry, Polly Walker, Maggie Smith, Frank Whaley, Valerie Perrine
Director: Peter Yates
Screenplay: Todd Alcott, from a story by Andrew S Karsch

After returning to form with *Little Voice*, Caine made *Curtain Call*, alongside his *California Suite* co-star Maggie Smith, for veteran director Peter Yates of *Bullitt* fame.

Caine and Smith play a dearly departed theatrical couple who once resided in a town house, now owned by a book publisher, played by James Spader. The duo come back as ghosts to wreak havoc in the house while doling out advice to Spader about his reluctance to marry a magazine editor. 'When I saw the script I went nuts,' said Caine during production. 'I mean we're two old actors and ghosts. We could just do what we liked – camp it up and do it over the top.'

The Debtors (1998) UNRELEASED

Randy Quaid, Michael Caine, Catherine McCormack
Director: Evi Quaid

The Debtors is a comedy about a group of dysfunctional individuals with various gambling addictions who meet up at the tables in Las Vegas. Caine plays a sex-addict dentist.

The movie reportedly cost $12.8 million and was financed by Microsoft's chief software architect Charles Simonyi. The billionaire was reportedly unhappy with the tone and content of the film, claiming it bore no resemblance to the picture he financed.

He gained an injunction against the film being shown, although director Evi Quaid went ahead and screened it at the Toronto Film Festival.

Get Carter (2000)

Thriller US Colour 102mins
Sylvester Stallone, Miranda Richardson, Rachael Leigh Cook, Rhona Mitra, Michael Caine
Director: Stephen Kay
Producer: Mark Canton
Screenplay: David McKenna based on the novel *Jack's Return Home* by Ted Lewis

Remakes always sound like bad news, and this Hollywood take on one of Britain's finest gangster movies borders on sacrilege. With Sly Stallone in the role of Jack Carter, Caine was persuaded to make a guest appearance. Producer Mark Canton was adamant that Caine appear somewhere in the picture: 'I'm a huge fan of Michael Caine. He is an actor that makes any role his own. His work in this film is the perfect complement to his work in the original.'

Caine was keen to take on the project, as he made clear during filming: 'I liked what they had done with it. When I played Carter, I was in Mafia terms a "made" man. I was one of the big guys. This Carter, on the other hand, is on the outside trying to get in. He is not so brutal. After all, the crusade he is on is a moral one. It's a much richer character that Sly is playing.'

Stallone seemed an odd choice for the lead, but nevertheless he reinvented the character, although the ghosts of the original lurking on set must have cramped his style: 'I did feel kind of odd,' said Stallone, 'because I have a couple of scenes with Michael where he starts to yell at me and then I have to say "No, you're a big man but you're way out of shape. With me it's a full time job. So please sit down and relax." I said to myself "My God! I'm threatening the original bad guy, Carter himself".'

The film was a box-office disaster, performing so badly that it didn't even receive a theatrical release in the UK, going straight to video.

Quicksand (2001) UNRELEASED

Michael Caine, Michael Keaton, Judith Godreche, Rade Serbedzija
Director: John Mackenzie
Producer: Geoffrey Reeve and Jim Reeve
Screenplay: Timothy Prager

Quicksand began production on the French Riviera in 2000 and by June 2003 had still not found international distribution. *Quicksand* was the third time Caine had teamed up with director John Mackenzie, previously collaborating on *The Honorary Consul* and *The Fourth Protocol*.

The workaholic head of the compliance section of a New York bank (Keaton) flies to Monaco to investigate unusual deposits from an offshore bank and meets a down-on-his-luck international film star (Caine) who has become embroiled in criminal activities.

Keaton remarked on his co-star's performance in *Premiere* magazine 'He always hits his mark. Sometimes he does so pretty hard. I was shocked. We do this funny fight scene and, you know, he's not 30 years old any more. This dude is strong!'

Financiers First Look Media screened the film at various festivals, but there are no plans for it to see the theatrical light of day.

Michael Caine
The Awards

Academy Awards

2003 Nominated Best Actor *The Quiet American*

2000 Won Best Supporting Actor *The Cider House Rules*

1987 Won Best Supporting Actor *Hannah And Her Sisters*

1984 Nominated Best Actor *Educating Rita*

1973 Nominated Best Actor *Sleuth*

1967 Nominated Best Actor *Alfie*

BAFTA Awards

2003 Nominated Best Actor *The Quiet American*

2000 Nominated Best Supporting Actor *The Cider House Rules*

1999 Nominated Best Actor *Little Voice*

1987 Nominated Best Actor *Hannah And Her Sisters*

1984 Won Best Actor *Educating Rita*

1984 Nominated Best Actor *The Honorary Consul*

Golden Globe Awards, USA

2003 Nominated Best Actor *The Quiet American*

2000 Nominated Best Supporting Actor *The Cider House Rules*

1999 Won Best Actor *Little Voice*

1998 Nominated Best Actor in a Mini-series *Mandela and De Klerk*

1991 Nominated Best Actor in a Mini-series *Jekyll and Hyde*

1989 Won Best Actor in a Mini-series *Jack The Ripper*

1989 Nominated Best Actor *Dirty Rotten Scoundrels*

1987 Nominated Best Supporting Actor *Hannah And Her Sisters*

1984 Won Best Actor

BAFTA/LA Awards

1992 Won Excellence in Film

British Independent Film Awards

1999 Nominated Best Actor *Little Voice*

Chicago Film Critics Association Awards

1999 Nominated Best Supporting Actor *Little Voice*

Emmy Awards

1997 Nominated Supporting Actor in a mini-series
Mandela and De Klerk

1994 Nominated Lead actor in a mini-series
World War II: When Lions Roared

1990 Nominated Lead actor in a mini-series
Jekyll & Hyde

Empire Awards UK

1999 Nominated Best British Actor
The Cider House Rules

2000 Won Lifetime Achievement Award

European Film Awards

2001 Nominated Best Actor *Last Orders*

Evening Standard British Film Awards

1999 Won Special Award For services not only
to British film, but also to international cinema

1975 Won Best Actor *Sleuth*

1966 2nd place New Face, Male *Alfie*

London Critics Circle Film Awards

2003 Won Best Actor *The Quiet American*

2001 Nominated Best Supporting Actor *Quills*

2000 Won Best Supporting Actor *Little Voice*

1998 Won Dilys Powell Award

National Board of Review, USA

2001 Won Best Ensemble Performance *Last Orders*

1998 Won Career Achievement Award

National Circle of Film Critics Awards, USA

1967 Won Best Actor *Alfie*

Golden Satellite Awards

2003 Won Best Actor *The Quiet American*

2000 Nominated Best Supporting Actor
The Cider House Rules

1999 Nominated Best Actor *Little Voice*

1998 Nominated Best Actor in a Mini-series
Mandela and De Klerk

San Francisco Film Critics Circle Awards

2002   Won Best Actor *The Quiet American*

San Sebastian International Film Festival

2000   Won Donostia lifetime Achievement Award

1996   Won Silver Seashell *Blood And Wine*

Screen Actors Guild Awards

2000   Won Best Supporting Actor *The Cider House Rules*

2000   Nominated Performance by a cast *The Cider House Rules*

1999   Nominated Performance by a cast *Little Voice*

Razzie Awards

1988   Nominated Worst Supporting Actor *Jaws: The Revenge*

1981   Nominated Worst Actor *Dressed To Kill*

Bibliography

What's It All About?, Michael Caine, Arrow 1993

Arise, Sir Michael Caine, William Hall, Blake Publishing 2001

Michael Caine, Michael Freedland, Orion 2000

My Name is Michael Caine: A Life in Film, Anne Billson, Frederick Muller 1991

Roger Moore, His Films and Career, Gareth Owen & Oliver Bayan, Robert Hale 2002

I would like to say a big thank-you to Gareth Owen & Oliver Bayan for allowing me to reproduce quotes from their book *Roger Moore: His Career and Films* (Hale)

Picture acknowledgments

We would like to thank all the film production and distribution companies and photographers whose publicity photographs appear in this book. We apologise in advance for any unintentional omission or neglect and will be pleased to insert the appropriate acknowledgement to any companies or individuals in any subsequent edition of this work.

Front Cover Kobal/MGM (Turner Ent.) ph: Bob Penn; **6 left** The Joel Finler Collection; **6 centre** BFI/Paramount; **6 right** The Joel Finler Collection; **7 left** The Joel Finler Collection; **7 centre** The Joel Finler Collection; **7 right** The Joel Finler Collection; **13** Kobal/Universal; **15** BFI/Paramount; **16** The Joel Finler Collection; **18/19** The Joel Finler Collection; **20** The Joel Finler Collection; **22** Kobal/Rank ph: George Courtney Ward; **23** The Joel Finler Collection; **24/25** The Joel Finler Collection; **26** Kobal/Sheldrake Films; **28** Kobal/Universal; **30** Kobal/Lowndes/Paramount; **33** Kobal/Sigma/ Paramount; **35** The Joel Finler Collection; **37** The Joel Finler Collection; **38** BFI/Paramount; **39** BFI/ Paramount; **41** Kobal/United Artists ph: Bob Penn; **43** Kobal/ABC/Season/Cinerama ph: John Jay; **44/45** Kobal/MGM (Turner Ent.) ph: Bob Penn; **46/47** Kobal/MGM (Turner Ent.) ph: Bob Penn; **49** The Joel Finler Collection; **51** Kobal/Palomar ph: George Whitear; **53** The Joel Finler Collection; **55** The Joel Finler Collection; **57** The Joel Finler Collection; **59** Kobal/National Film Trustee Co./Arlington Pictures ph: Barrie Payne; **61** Kobal/Columbia/Devon Co. ph: Ian Coates; **62** The Joel Finler Collection; **65** The Joel Finler Collection; **67** Kobal/Warner Bros. ph: John Monte; **69** Kobal/Columbia/Rastar Films ph: Mel Traxel; **71** Kobal/Beverly Films; **73** The Joel Finler Collection; **75** The Joel Finler Collection; **77** The Joel Finler Collection; **78/79** Kobal/Victory/Lorimar/ Paramount; **81** Kobal/Orion; **83** The Joel Finler Collection; **85** The Joel Finler Collection; **86** The Joel Finler Collection; **89** Kobal/Parsons & Whittemore Lyddon/Paramount ph: Clive Coote; **90** The Joel Finler Collection; **93** The Joel Finler Collection; **94** The Ronald Grant Archive/Courtesy Orion Pictures; **97** Kobal/Handmade Films ph: Clive Coote; **99** Kobal/Handmade Films ph: Clive Coote; **100** The Joel Finler Collection; **103** Kobal/Fourth Protocol Dist. ph: Bob Penn; **105** Kobal/ITC Ent. (Carlton Int.) ph: Graham Attwood; **107** Kobal/Orion ph: Bob Penn; **109** Kobal/21st Century Prod; **111** Kobal/Touchstone/ Amblin ph: Ron Batzdorff; **112/113** Kobal/Jim Henson prods. ph: Richard Blanshard; **114** Kobal/Harry Palmer Prod/Showtime ph: Piroska Mihalka; **117** Kobal/20th century Fox ph: Glenn Watson; **119** Kobal/Miramax/Scala Prods. ph: Laurie Sparham; **121** Kobal/Miramax ph: Stephen Vaughan; **122** Kobal/Miramax ph: Stephen Vaughan; **125** Kobal 20th Century Fox ph: David Appleby; **127** The Ronald Grant Archive/Courtesy Geoff Reeves Films; **128/129** Kobal/Castle Rock/ Fortis/ WV Films ph: Ron Batzdorff; **130/131** Kobal/Scala/MBP ph: Simon Mein; **133** Kobal/New Line pg: Melinda Sue Gordon; **135** Kobal/IMF/Miramax/Co. ph: Phil Bray; **136** Kobal/IMF/Miramax/ Co. ph: Phil Bray; **138** Miramax.

Author acknowledgements

I would like to acknowledge and thank:

Ann Jenkin (Michael Caine's office)
Lady Shakira Caine
Sir Michael Caine (for his enthusiasm and support for the project)

I would like to say a big thank you to my commissioning editor Tina Persaud, whose focus and guidance made this book possible.

My friends and family have been hugely supportive, and in particular I would like to mention: Ben Cannon, Kathryn Corbin, Maureen Cowle, Rhian Dickeson, Andrew Field, James Head, Mark Laycock, Sue Martin, Alison Martin, Jonathan Mapplebeck, Carl May, Darren May, Jason May, Jessica May, Richard Moran, my grandmother Josephine Neal, Harry Neal, Simon Paris, Yvonne Roy, Lucy and Irene Sahandi, Dave Sillett, Nigel Sillett, Susan 'Chief' Sillett, William Smallwood, Matthew Smith, Brian and Barbara Spreadbury, Neil Spreadbury, Suzanne Tait, Louise Turnley, Ceri Taylor, Melissa Vincent, Christopher and Karen Warner, Robert Way, Mark Wilson, and Steven Wrench.

My whole-hearted thanks also go to: Lancelot Narayan for your help and support, but in particular your appreciation of *Blue Ice*!; Ajay Chowdhury for your encouragement, excitement, support and advice; Michael Deeley, my mentor. Tony Gould for introducing me to *Educating Rita*; Claire Kendall-Price for inspiration at the darkest hours; Graham Rye for introducing me to the world of writing; my tutors and friends at Bournemouth University; my Mum and Dad who support and encourage me in everything I do.

Index

Folios in **bold** indicate a main entry
Folios in *italics* indicate a photograph